ELEGANCE OF ENGLISH

KAPPIYA CLASSICS

Contents

Contents

Foreword

KAPPIYA CLASSICS

Hello Dear Readers

I am Tamizhiniya Tamizhdesan

when I was studying in school my teachers used to conduct lessons between many good books and that conduct gave me confidence that I can conduct more than a hundred topics with introductory speech. My Technical education helped a lot in this aspect. When I became a teacher I assisted my students in the way our teachers guided us.

My school, college and workplace friends lives scattered in different countries, the families of them too scattered in different nation, whereas I live in the Land of my Mother Language(Tamilnadu). Among my friends who are running to strive for their living, I have selected the publishing department to read their lives and pass it on to others. We are publishing legendary works under Kappiya Vasipagam. So far we have published more than 1500 books in package type.

I have used the library a lot in my school, college and work life. Novelist Vasu Murugavel writes that he brought a bundle of books from a person, read them and returned them. Similarly, I have imported hundreds of books read them and sent them back. I have also written novel in Tamil and English, also a book based on the Culture of Tamil People.

My son Imayakappiyan (8) started learning his Tamil lettering from the texts of our cover pages. The same way he is gaining the knowledge of book names, authors also the technical knowledge in publishing and helps us in many ways. My husband Tamizhdesan guides me about the packaging materials of the book contents and his creative thinking of book cover page makes me to create some unique cover pages. We three feel very happy to be in this field which makes us to learn continuously.

CHAPTER I

The Greatest Language of the World

English is The Greatest Language of the World. Of some three thousand existing languages, large and small, English is second only to Chinese in number of speakers. It has well over 300 million native speakers, plus probably as many more who handle it in pidgin fashion or as an acquired tongue. It enjoys the widest distribution of any language on earth, appearing in numerous countries on every continent as an official tongue and unofficially in many more over half of the world's scientific publications, books, newspapers and magazines are entirely or partly in English. In international congresses and gatherings, English is used more often than any other tongue. More than half of the world's radio and television programs are in English and it is the language most commonly used in the world's airways and seaways.

A was an archer who shot at a frog.
B was a butcher and kept a great dog.
C was a captain all covered with lace.
D was a drunkard and had a red face.
E was an esquire with insolent brow.
F was a farmer and followed the plough.
G was a gamester who had but ill-luck.
H was a hunter and hunting a buck.
I was an inkeeper who loved to bouse.
J was a joiner and built up a house;
K was a King William once governed this land.
L was a lady who had a white hand.
M was a miser, and hoarded up gold;
N was a nobleman gallant and bold.
O was an oyster, wench and went about town.
P was a parson and wore a black gown.
Q was a queen who was fond of flip.
R was a robber, and wanted a whip.
S was a sailor and spent all he got.
T was a tinker and mended a pot.
U was a usurer a miserable elf.

V was a vinter who drank all himself.
W was a watchman and guarded the door.
X was a expensive and so became poor.
Y was a youth who did not love school.
Z was a zany, a silly old fool.

A Curious Discourse

This is a A Curious Discourse that passed between the Twenty-Five Letters at Dinner-Time.

Says **A**, give me a good large slice.
Says **B**, a little bit, but nice.
Says **C**, cut me a piece of crust.
Take it, says **D**, it's dry as dust.
Says **E**, I'll cut fast, who will.
Says **F**, I vow I'll home my fill.
Says **G**, give it me good and great.
Says **H**, a little bit I hate.
Says **I**, I have the juice the best.
And **K**, the very same confest.
Says **L**, ther's nothing more I love.
Says **M**, it makes your teeth to move.
N noticed what the others said.
O other's plates with grief survey'd.
P praised that took up to the life.
Q quarrell'd Cause he'd a bad knife.
Says **R**, it runs short, I'am afraid.
S silent sat and nothing said.
T thought that talking might lose time
U understood it at meals a crime.
W wish'd these had been a quince in;
Says **X**, those cooks ther's no convincing.
Says **Y**, I'll eat, let others wish.
Z sat as mute as any fish, While Ampersy and he licked the dish.

CHAPTER II

Verbalising Faculty of English

Envy we must those bards who compose in Italian or German:

Apposite Feminine Rhymes give them no bother at all.

We, though, thanks, to a Tongue deprived of so many inflexions,

Can very easily turn nouns, if we wish, into verbs.
   Animal------Cry

1.   Apes------------gibber
2.   ases------------bray
3.   bees------------hum
4.   beetles------------drone
5.   bears------growl
6.   bitterns------boom
7.   blackbirds------whistle
8.   blackcaps------we speak of the"chick-chick" of the blackcap
9.   bulls------bellow
10.   canaries------sing or quaver
11.   cats------mew, purr, swear, and caterwaul
12.   calves------bleat and blear
13.   chaffinches------chirp or pink
14.   chickens------pip
15.   cicadæs------sing
16.   cocks------crow
17.   cows------moo or low
18.   crows------caw
19.   cuckoos------cry, cuckoo
20.   deer------bell
21.   dogs------bark, bay, howl, and yelp

22. doves------coo
23. ducks------quack
24. eagles-----cream
25. falcons------chant
26. flies------buzz
27. foxes------bark and yelp
28. frogs------croak
29. geese------cackle and hiss
30. goldfinch------we speak of the "merry twinkle" of the female
31. grasshoppers------chirp and pitter
32. grouse------we speak of the "drumming" of the grouse
33. guineafowls------cry "come back"
34. guineapigss------queak
35. hares------queak
36. hawks------cream
37. hens------cackle and cluck
38. horses------neigh and whinny
39. hyenas------laugh
40. jays------chatter
41. kittens------mew
42. lambs------baa and bleat
43. larks------sing
44. linnets------chuckle in their call
45. lions------roar
46. magpies------chatter
47. mices------queak and squeal
48. monkeys------chatter and gibber
49. nightingales------pipe and warble—we also speak of its "jug-jug"
50. owls------hoot and screech
51. oxen------low and bellow
52. parrots------talk
53. peacocks------cream
54. peewits------cry "pee-wit"
55. pigeons------coo
56. pigs------grunt, squeak, and squeal
57. ravens------croak
58. reds------tarts whistle
59. rooks------caw

60. screech-owls------creech or shriek
61. sheep------baa or bleat
62. snakes------hiss
63. sparrows------chirp or yelp
64. stags------bellow and call
65. swallows------twitter
66. swans------cry—we also speak of the "bombilation" of the swan
67. thrushes------whistle
68. tigers------growl
69. tits------we speak of the "twittwit" of the bottle-tit
70. turkey-cocks------gobble
71. vultures------cream
72. whitethroats------chirr
73. wolves------howl

CHAPTER III

Punctuation is Everything

The Society for Editors and Proofreaders (SfEP), in association with the BBC News website Magazine, challenged readers to write a thank you letter with two meanings.. Just use the same words - or words that sound the same - but change the punctuation. It's harder than you think!

Here are some of the entries received:

Letter - 1

Dear Mother,

In law, there is nothing to make me say thank you, but the quality of your gifts compels me at least to write to tell you how I feel. Thank you so much for the presents! I was expecting nothing more than a token yet, again, you have exceeded even your own incredible standards.

It was a shame you had to stay here for such a short time. I thought I might have coped, but it was unbearable seeing you leave. The relief was immense when I heard we might see you again soon. I wanted to end it all by saying goodbye now. I hope I will not have to say it to you again for a long time. If you have the opportunity to spend Christmas elsewhere next year, please do not.

Much love

Matthew

Dear Mother-in-Law,

There is nothing to make me say thank you, but the quality of your gifts compels me at least to write to tell you how I feel. Thank you? So much for the presents I was expecting. Nothing more than a token, yet again! You have exceeded even your own incredible standards.

It was a shame you had to stay here. For such a short time, I thought I might have coped, but it was unbearable. Seeing you leave, the relief was immense. When I heard we might see you again soon, I wanted to end it all. By saying goodbye now, I hope I will not have to say it to you again for a long time. If you have the opportunity to spend Christmas elsewhere next year, please do.

Not much love

Matthew

Letter 2

Dear Mandy,

Just a quick note to say I received your gift - I was very surprised! When I saw the effort you had gone to I nearly cried. When I heard that you were coming for our roast turkey lunch I looked forward to the Christmas day celebration far more. Disdaining others no doubt spending the festive season feeling drunk, with joy we sang the classic yuletide carols. However, the horror on the streets tonight - revellers ignore the message of Christmas and down pints instead - I wish I could be there to help them.

Clair.

Dear Mandy,

Just a quick note to say I received your gift - I was very surprised when I saw the effort you had gone to. I nearly cried when I heard that you were coming for our roast turkey lunch. I looked forward to a Christmas day celebration far more disdaining. Others no doubt spending the festive season feeling drunk with joy - we sang the classic yuletide carols, however. The horror. On the streets tonight revellers ignore the message of Christmas and down pints instead. I wish I could be there to help them.

Clair

Letter 3

Dear Santa,

You really made my year! When I heard you had fallen from your sleigh, I was sad. To see such wonderful gifts lined up under my Christmas tree, my eyes lit up. When I unwrapped your gifts I knew that the spirit of Christmas was still alive. It was terrible hearing about your accident. The best piece of news all year is your safe return. Things yet to come, you say! Christmas is a time to love and share, I disagree with Scrooges. Everywhere Christmas is slowly fading. Thanks for making it so fantastic.

Matt

Dear Santa,

You really made my year when I heard you had fallen from your sleigh! I was sad to see such wonderful gifts lined up under my Christmas tree. My eyes lit up when I unwrapped your gifts. I knew the spirit of Christmas was still alive - it was terrible. Hearing about your accident? The best piece of news all year. Is your safe return a sign of things yet to come? You say Christmas is a time to love and share, I disagree. With Scrooges everywhere, Christmas is slowly fading. Thanks for making it so. Fantastic.

Matt.

Letter - 4

Dear Auntie Maude,

I was amazed to receive yet again the perfumed soap you've compelled me to appreciate for three straight Christmases! That my family had suffered due to my body odour, I felt such delight. I took the soap to the bathroom. I normally enter only once each July, not that I wish to. Wash? Never! Could a mere gift change that? No! Your stubbornness fuelled my resolve. To drive my body to the soapy unknown, my family have sued me for cruelty, and threatened random hose attacks. I cannot allow that water and skin should meet.

With dignity intact!

Rob

Dear Auntie Maude,

I was amazed to receive yet again the perfumed soap. You've compelled me to appreciate, for three straight Christmases, that my family had suffered due to my body odour. I felt such delight, I took the soap to the bathroom I normally enter only once each July! Not that I wish to wash. Never could a mere gift change that. No, your stubbornness fuelled my resolve to drive my body to the soapy unknown. My family have sued me for cruelty, and threatened random hose attacks. I will not allow that. Water and skin should meet with dignity intact.

Rob

Letter 5

Dear Aunt Agatha,

Sorry it has taken me so long to write telling you how much I liked your Christmas present this year, only I didn't have the time. To take it back and get another would be out of the question! I suppose for you to be so kind shouldn't come as a surprise after what you bought me last year. It was splendid! News about Uncle Brian? Dying to see you again in the New Year. Would be awful to lose touch.

Mark

Dear Aunt Agatha,

Sorry it has taken me so long to write telling you how much I liked your Christmas present this year, only I didn't. Have the time to take it back and get another? Would be out of the question, I suppose, for you to be so kind.

Shouldn't come as a surprise after what you bought me last year. It was splendid news about Uncle Brian dying. To see you again in the New Year would be awful.

To lose touch,
Mark

Letter 6
Dear Aunty Grace,

What a surprise to receive a nice gift from you when I had not sent you my new address. I had thought you would not be able to send a present this year.

Wasting good money at this time of year, it is common for people to send presents that are far too big, like those giant toy clowns.

You always insist on sending me great presents, like this year's. Our incredible walks on Xmas day were particularly fun this year. Without you too much food and drink was consumed in haste.

Rebecca

Dear Aunty Grace,

What a surprise! To receive a nice gift from you! When I had not sent you my new address I had thought you would not be able to send a present this year - wasting good money. At this time of year it is common for people to send presents that are far too big, like those giant toy clowns you always insist on sending me. Great presents like this year's are incredible! Walks on Xmas day were particularly fun this year without you. Too much food and drink was consumed.

In haste,

Rebecca
Punctuation is everything!

CHAPTER IV

Misinterpretation

In the days when you couldn't count on a public toilet facility, an English woman was planning a trip to India. She was registered to stay in a small guest house owned by the local schoolmaster. She was concerned as to whether the guest house contained a WC. In England, as you know, a bathroom is commonly called a WC which stands for "Water Closet". She wrote to the schoolmaster inquiring of the facilities about the WC.

The school master, not fluent in English, asked the local priest if he knew the meaning of WC. Together they pondered possible meanings of the letters and concluded that the lady wanted to know if there was a "Wayside Chapel " (Place where Celebrations are done especially like a beautiful garden) near the house . . . a bathroom never entered their minds.

So the schoolmaster wrote the following reply:

Dear Madam,

I take great pleasure in informing you that the WC is located 9 miles from the house. It is located in the middle of a grove of pine trees, surrounded by lovely grounds. It is capable of holding 229 people and is open on Sundays and Thursdays. As there are many people expected in the summer months, I suggest you arrive early. There is, however, plenty of standing room. This is an unfortunate situation especially if you are in the habit of going regularly. It may be of some interest to you that my daughter was married in the WC as it was there that she met her husband. It was a wonderful event. There were 10 people in every seat. It was wonderful to see the expressions on their faces. We can take photos in different angle.

My wife, sadly, has been ill and unable to go recently. It has been almost a year since she went last, which pains her greatly. You will be pleased to know that many people bring their lunch and make a day of it. Others prefer to wait till the last minute and arrive just in time. I would recommend Your Ladyship plan to go on a Thursday as there is an organ accompaniment. The acoustics are excellent and even the most delicate sounds can be heard everywhere. The newest addition is a bell which rings every time a person enters. We are holding a bazaar to provide plush seats for all since many feel it is long needed. I look forward to escorting you there myself and seating you in a place where you can be seen by all.

CHAPTER V

Heart of the Matter

Since ancient times, the heart has been an integral part of life, love and lore. In fact think of love and the first symbol that comes to mind is a red heart. Naturally the heart has been the subject of and the inspiration for hundreds of songs and thousands of poems, which has helped millions to 'win the hearts' of the ones that they have 'given their hearts' to.

What is interesting is that the English language too is indebted to the heart. Of the 400 or so phrases related to the human body, the heart pumps life into more than 50 of them.

Here are some heart-y phrases with their meaning. Of course the list is not all-inclusive.

1. A heart of gold – good-natured, caring, forgiving.
2. A heart of stone – cruel, ruthless, without feeling.
3. Absence makes the heart grow fonder – not being with someone or something makes it more desirable (Francis Davidson's Poetical Rhapsody, 1602).
4. After one's own heart – someone liked for having similar feelings, interests or ideas.
5. An affair of the heart – to be in love and not just be attracted physically.
6. As tender as a mother's heart – very kind.
7. At heart – in actuality.
8. Be still my heart – asking oneself to not get too excited.
9. Big hearted – kind and generous.
10. Break one's heart – someone or something that makes one sad.
11. Change of heart – change in the way one thinks or feels.
12. Cold hands warm heart – a kind hearted person but with a reserved exterior.
13. Cross my heart and hope to die – to promise that what one has said is true.
14. Cry / eat / sob your heart out – grieve hopelessly.
15. Dagger in the heart – create a feeling of defeat or hopelessness.

16. Faint heart never won fair lady – one should not be timid in the matter of love (and even life).

17. From the bottom of my heart – with a lot of sincerity.

18. Get to the heart of the matter – figure out the most important thing about something.

19. Give heart to – fall in love with.

20. Harden your heart – to make immune one's feelings.

21. Have a heart – to request someone to be kind.

22. Heart breaker – someone or something that makes you sad.

23. Heart goes out to – feels sorry for.

24. Heart is in the right place – kind-hearted.

25. Heart rending – causing grief.

26. Heart stands still – be very frightened or worried.

27. Heartthrob – sweetheart.

28. Heart to heart talk – talk about some serious and intimate matter in great detail.

29. Heart warming – very pleasing.

30. Heart's delight – to one's satisfaction.

31. Heavy heart – weighed down with sorrow.

32. Learn by heart – memorize.

33. Lose heart – feel discouraged because of failure.

34. Lose your heart – fall in love.

35. Melt the heart – get sentimental.

36. My heart bleeds – be very sad.

37. Near and dear to my heart / near to one's heart – very close to one.

38. Open one's heart – talk honestly about one's feelings to someone.

39. Put your heart into – do something with great enthusiasm.

40. Search one's heart – try and discover the reason for our thoughts and actions.

41. Set one's heart on – resolve to get or achieve something important.

42. Skip a beat – be startled due to surprise or fear.

43. Steal someone's heart – make someone fall in love with.

44. Sweetheart – the one that you love.

45. Take heart – be encouraged and try again.

46. The way to a man's heart is through his stomach – an old saying probably from the time when women looked after the house and to be able to cook well was important to get a good husband.

47. Tugging at heartstrings – playing on one's emotions.

48. Warms the cockles of my heart – someone or something that delights, comforts, warms and brings a sentimental feeling.

49. Wear one's heart on one's sleeves – show one's feelings openly without fear or embarrassment (origin: from ancient times when a young man pursuing a girl would assert his love for her by wearing her name on his sleeve).

50. Win the heart of – win the love / affection of.

51. With all my heart – with great sincerity.

52. Young at heart – to be youthful & zestful, irrespective of age.

CHAPTER VI

Funny facts

'**Lollipop**' is the longest word typed With your right hand.

There are two words in the English language that have all five vowels in order: '**abstemious**' **and** '**facetious.**'

TYPEWRITER is the longest word that can be made using the letters only on one row of the keyboard.

"**Almost**" is the longest word in the English language with all the letters in alphabetical order.

"**Rhythm**" is the longest English word without a vowel.

'**Stewardesses**' is the longest word that is typed with only the left hand.

There is only ONE word in the English language with THREE CONSECUTIVE SETS OF DOUBLE LETTERS.... **Bookkeeper**

There is a word in the English language with only one vowel, which occurs five times: "**indivisibility.**"

There is a seven letter word in the English language that contains ten words without rearranging any of its letters, "**therein**": the, there, he, in, rein, her, here, ere, therein, herein.

There are only 4 words in the English language which end in "duos": **tremendous, horrendous, stupendous,** and **hazardous.**

The shortest word in the English language with all its letters in alphabetical order is the word "**almost**"

The letter most in use in the English language is "E" and the letter "Q" is least used.

Out of all the eight letter words in the English language, only one has only one vowel in it: "**strength**"

Only 3 words in the English language end in "ceed": "**proceed**", "**exceed**" **and** "**succeed.**"

Of all the languages in the world, English has the largest vocabulary about **800,000 words.**

"**Forty**" is the only number which has its letters in alphabetical order. "**One**" is the only number with its letters in reverse alphabetical order.

"**Four**" is the only number whose number of letters in the name equals the number./The most common letters in English are **R S T L N E.**

"**Go**" is the shortest complete sentence in the English language.

CHAPTER VII

Beautiful Expressions

There are innumerable beautiful expressions in English. **A thing of beauty is a joy for ever** is one of the immortal lines of the great poet **Keats**.

The Beauty is ultimate reality is another immortal lines but of **Tagore**. The English language abounds in such beautiful expressions which bring us immense joy. Happy turns of phrases, striking imageries, peculiar styles, semantically interesting structures and memorable phrases are added in this page.

Here are few of those immortal lines and beautiful expressions.

1. Adventure is the champagne of life. (*G. K. Chesterton*)
2. Adversity's sweet milk is philosophy. (*Romeo and Juliet 3: 3: 55*)
3. All do not all things well. (*Thomas Champion*)
4. All experience is an arch to build upon. (*Henry Brooks Adams*)
5. All is at once sunk in their whirl-pool death. (*Donne*)
6. All things to end are made. (*Thomas Nashe*)
7. The almighty dollar is the only object of worship. (*Anon*)
8. Ambition should be made of sterner stuff. (*Julius Caesar 3:2:97*)
9. And death shall be no more. death, thou shalt die. (*Donne*)
10. And justify the ways of God of men. (*Paradise Lost 1 – 22*)
11. And nature must obey necessity. (*Julius Caesar 4:3:225*)
12. And purer than the purest gold. (*Ben Jonson : The Touchstone of Truth*)
13. Apt words have power to suage the tumors of a troubled mind. (*Milton Samson 1.184*)
14. Art is man added to nature. (*Bacon*)
15. Art lies in concealing art. (*Latin Proverb*)
16. As good luck would have it. (*Merry Wives 3: 5: 86*)
17. Atheism is a theoretical formulation of the discouraged life. (*Hendry Emerson Fosdick*)
18. Bad's the best of us. (*Beaumont and Fletcher. The Bloody Brother 4-2*)
19. The ballot is stronger than the bullet. (*Abraham Lincoln*)
20. Bankrupt of life, yet prodigal of ease. (*Dryden : Absalom 168*)
21. A barren superfluity of words. (*Sir Samuel Garth*)
22. Beauty's sweet but beauty's frail. (*Thomas Carew*)

23. The best doctors in the world are Doctor Diet, Doctor Quiet, and Doctor Merry man. (*Swift : Polite Conversation*)
24. The best is yet to be. (*Browning*)
25. Better than the best. (*Paradise Lost 1 - 262*)
26. Better to reign in hell than serve in heaven. (*Paradise Lost 1-262*)
27. Brief is life but love is long. (*Tennyson*)
28. The busy candidates for power and fame. (*Dr. Johnson*)
29. Care - charming Sleep, thou easer of all woes, Brother to death. (*Beaumont and Fletcher*)
30. The child is father of the man. (*Wordsworth*)
31. To choose time is to save time. (*Bacon Essays*)
32. Cunning is the dark sanctuary of incapacity. (*Chesterfield*)
33. Danger comes in silence and in secret. (*Isaac Pocock*)
34. Dark with excessive bright. (*Paradise Lost : 3 – 380*)
35. A day is miniature eternity. (*Emerson: Journals*)
36. Death be not proud, though some have called thee. (*Donne*)
37. Death hath so many doors to let out life. (*Beaumont and Fletcher*)
38. The custom of the country. (*2-2*)
39. Deeds, not words shall speak me. (*Beanmont and Fletcher : The Lover's Progress 3-6*)
40. Do you think I am easier to be played on than a pipe? (*Hamlet 3-2-393*)
41. Earth laughs in flowers. (*Emerson*)
42. Eternal sunshine of the spotless mind. (*Pope*)
43. Even God can not change the past. (*Agathon*)
44. Evermore thanks, the exchequer of the poor. (*Goethe*)
45. Excessive scruple is only hidden pride. (*Goethe*)
46. Faint heart wins not lady fair. (*William James Linton*)
47. The fairest things have the fleetest end. (*F. Thomson*)
48. Faith is love taking the form of aspiration. (*William Ellery Channing*)
49. Fame is food that dead men eat. (*A. Dopson*)
50. A fanatic is one who can't change his mind and won't change the subject. (*Winston Churchill*)
51. Faultily faultless, icily regular, splendidly null, Dead perfection, no more. (*Tennyson*)
52. The fault's not in the object, but their eyes. (*Ben Jonson in Authorem*)
53. And feel that I am happier than I Know. (*Paradise Lost 8-282*)
54. For every why, he had a wherefore. (*Samuel Butler*)

55. For her own person, It beggar'd all description. (*Antony and Cleopatra : 2-2-199*)
56. For love is lust and life is a dream of death. (*James Elroy Flecker*)
57. For men may come and men may go, But I go on forever. (*Tennyson. The Brook. St. 6*)
58. For who would bear the whips and scorns of time. (*Hamlet 3:1:70*)
59. Friends are born, not made. (*Hendry Brooks Adams*)
60. From softness only softness comes. (*Marcus Curtius*)
61. Give it an understanding, but no tongue. (*Hamlet 1: 2: 249*)
62. God became man, that men might become God. (*St. Augustine*)
63. A good book is the precious life blood of a master spirit, embalmed and treasured upon purpose to a life beyond life. (*Milton : Aeropagitica*)
64. A good face is a letter of recommendation. (*Joseph Addison*)
65. Hail wedded love, mysterious law, true source of human offspring. (*Paradise Lost 4-750*)
66. Happiness is the shadow of thing past. (*Paradise Lost 4-299*)
67. He for God only. She for God in him. (*Paradise Lost 4-299*)
68. He was not of an age, but for all time. (*Ben Jonson*)
69. He wears the rose of youth upon him. (*Antony & Cleopatra 3 : 11 : 20*)
70. He, who will not when he may, may not when he will. (*John of Salisbury*)
71. Heaven lies about us in our infancy. (*Wordsworth*)
72. Heard melodies are sweet, but those unheard are sweeter. (*Keats*)
73. Heaven is our heritage, Earth but a player's stage. (*Thomas Nashe*)
74. A heaven on earth. (*Paradise Lost 4-208*)
75. The heart is not a clock, it will not wind again. (*Sacheverell Sitwell*)
76. Hector is dead. There is no more to say. (*Troilus & Cressida 5-10-22*)
77. Hills whose heads touch heaven. (*Othello 1 : 3: 141*)
78. Him first, him last, him midst, and without end. (*Paradise Lost 5-165*)
79. His time is forever, everywhere his place. (*Abraham Cowley*)
80. An honest man's the noble work of God.
81. Honest labour bears a lovely face. (*Thomas Dekker*)
82. How noiseless falls the foot of time. (*W. R. Spencer*)
83. Hypocrisy in the homage that vice offers to virtue. (*La Rochefaocauld*)
84. I am not in the roll of common men. (*Henry IV PTI 3 : 1 : 43*)
85. I am that I am. (*Exodus 3: 14*)
86. I am the master of my fate. I am the captain of my soul. (*William Ernest Henley*)
87. I can resist everything except temptation. (*Oscar Wilde*)

88. I grew intoxicated with my own eloquence. (*Disraeli*)
89. I have immortal longings in me. (*Antony & Cleopatra 5 : 2 : 282*)
90. I have touch'd the highest point of all my greatness. (*Henry VIII 3 : 2: 224*)
91. I love not Man the less, but Nature more. (*Byron : Childe Harold*)
92. I shall temper so justice with mercy. (*Paradise Lost 9 – 77*)
93. I want what I want when I want it. (*Henry Blossom*)
94. I was in the middle of the stream and must sink or swim. (*Hazlitt*)
95. I would be married to a single life. (*Richard Crashaw*)
96. Ice and iron can be welded. (*R. L. Stevenson*)
97. If summer come not, how can winter go? (*Richard Crashaw*)
98. If the worst comes to the worst.
99. It is better to be Socrates in prison than Caliban on the throne. (*Wil Durant*)
100. Jack of all trades and master of none.
101. Jack is common to all that will play.
102. If Jack's in love he's no judge' of Jill's beauty.
103. Joy delights joy.
104. Joy is a great medicine.
105. A just war is better than an unjust peace.
106. Justice delayed is justice denied.
107. Be just before you are generous.
108. Kings must have slaves.
109. The king's name is tower of strength.
110. Kindness is never wasted.
111. Kindness comes of will.
112. Keep your shop and your shop will keep you.
113. Language is the dress of thought. (*Dr. Johnson*)
114. Large was his health, but larger was his heart. (*Dryden : Absalom 1.826*)
115. The law allows it and the court awards it. (*Merchant of Venice 4 : 1 : 303*)
116. Law is the bottomless pit. (*John Arbuthnot*)
117. Laws grind the poor and rich men rule the law. (*Goldsmith*)
118. Let bus do or die. (*Robert Burns*)
119. Liberty! Equality! Fraternity!
120. Liquid lapse of murmuring streams. (*Paradise Lost : 8 – 263*)
121. A Little learning is dangerous thing. (*Pope*)
122. Love comforteth like sunshine after rain. (*Venus and Adonis 1-799*)
123. Love has found out a way to Live by Dying. (*John Dryden*)

124. Love is love's reward. (*John Dryden*)
125. Love's the noblest frailty of the mankind. (*John Dryden*)
126. Love is the perfect sum of all delight. (*Tobias Hume*)
127. Love makes all things equal. (*Shelley*)
128. Love will find out the way.
129. Make temples of my hears to God we must. (*Lord Brooke*)
130. Man delights not me, no not women neither. (*Hamlet 2: 2: 328*)
131. A man is good in ruin. (*Emerson*)
132. Man is a rope stretched between the animal and the superman. (*Nietzsche*)
133. Man is not merely an evolution but rather a revolution. (*G K. Chesterton*)
134. Man is the only animal that blushes or needs to.
135. Marriage has many pains, but celibacy has no pleasures. (*Johnson*)
136. May you live all the days of your life? (*Swift*)
137. A maxim consists of a minimum of sound and a maximum of sense. (*Mark Twain*)
138. Memory, the warder of the brain. (*Macheth 1 : 7: 65*)
139. Men are always sincere. They change sincerities, that's all. (*Tristan Bernard*)
140. A mind content both crown and kingdom is. (*Robert Greene*)
141. The moan of doves in immemorial elms.
142. And murmuring of innumerable bees. (*Tennyson*)
143. Money is like a sixth sense without which you cannot make a complete use of the other five. (*Somerset Maugham*)
144. Money speaks sense in a language all nations understand. (*Aphra Sehn*)
145. A moon, the eye of light, the star of wars. (*Aeschylus*)
146. Nature is the art of God Eternal. (*Dante*)
147. Never complain and never explain. (*Disraeli*)
148. None but the brave deserves the fair. (*J. Dryden*)
149. Now join your hands and with your hands your hearts. (*Henry IV pt 3. 4 : 6: 39*)
150. Now this is not the end. It is not even the beginning of the end. But it is, perhaps the end of the beginning. (*Winston Churchill*)
151. One touch of nature makes the whole world kin. (*Troilus & Cressida 3 : 3 : 171*)
152. The only thing we have to fear is fear itself. (*F D. Roosevelt*)
153. An ornament to her profession. (*John Bunyan*)
154. Our birth is but a sleep and a forgetting. (*Wordsworth*)

155. The path of duty was the way to glory. (*Tennyson*)
156. The pit of hell is as deep as despair. (*Abbot William*)
157. A place for everything and everything in its place.
158. Plain living and high thinking. (*Wordsworth*)
159. Pleasure is deaf when told of future pain. (*Cowper*)
160. Poetry is criticism of life. (*M. Arnold*)
161. A politician .... one that would circumvent God. (*Hamlet 5: 1 : 84*)
162. Politicians have no politics. (*G.K.Chesterton*)
163. Prayer is conversation with God.
164. Pride will spit in pride's face. (*Thomas Fuller*)
165. Progress is not mere movement, but it is improvement. (*L. S. N. Sarma*)
166. Promise made is a debt unpaid. (*Robert William Service*)
167. Prosperity makes friends, adversity tries them. (*Publius Syrus*)
168. The quite mind is richer than crown. (*Robert Greeny*)
169. The remedy is worse than the disease. (*Bacon*)
170. The river glideth at his own sweet will. (*Wordsworth*)
171. In a rudderless boat upon the vastness of the Infinite. (*Sri Aurobindo*)
172. Sadder than sorrow : sweeter than delight. (*C. Patmore*)
173. See golden days, fruitful of golden deeds. (*Paradise Lost 3-337*)
174. She was perfect past all parallel. (*Bayron*)
175. The shirt of Nessus is upon me. (*Antony & Cleopatra 4 : 10 : 56*)
176. The shortest answer is doing. (*Lord Herbert*)
177. The silence that is in the starry sky, the sleep that is among the lonely hills. (*Wordsworth*)
178. Sing away sorrow. Cast away care. (*Cervantes*)
179. A soft embalmer of the still midnight. (*John Keats : To Sleep*)
180. Some folks are wise and some are otherwise. (*Smollet, Tobies*)
181. Some people are more nice than wise. (*Cowper*)
182. Sound etymology has nothing to do with sound. (*Max Muller*)
183. Steep'd me in poverty to the very lips. (*Othello 4 : 2 : 49*)
184. (Lucy Gray) The sweetest thing that ever grew beside a human door. (*Wordsworth*)
185. The sweets of love are mixed with tears. (*Robert Herrick*)
186. The sum of earthly bliss. (*Paradise Lost 8-522*)
187. Superstition is the religion of feeble minds. (*Burke*)
188. Suspense in news is a torture. (*Milton Samson 1 – 1569*)
189. There is a divinity that shapes our end. (*Shakespeare*)
190. There's a special providence in the fall of a sparrow. (*Hamlet 5-2-232*)

191.   There is danger in delay. (*Giles Fletcher*)

192.   There is nothing either good or bad. But thinking makes it so. (*Hamlet 2 – 2 -259*)

193.   There is nothing great or small. (*E. B. Browning*)

194.   This only I know that I know not the things which I cannot know. (*St. Ambrose*)

195.   This was the most unkindest cut of all. (*Julius Caesar 3: 2: 188*)

196.   Those thoughts that wander through eternity. (*Paradise Lost 2-147*)

197.   Thou wander'st in the labyrinth of life. (*Dryden*)

198.   Thou wert my guide, philosopher and friend. (*Pope*)

199.   Thou life is short, let us not make it so. (*Ben Jonson*)

200.   Thoughts that breathe and words that burn. (*Gray*)

201.   Thus conscience does make cowards of us all. (*Hamlet 3 : 1 : 83*)

202.   Time alone doth change and last. (*John Ford*)

203.   Time fleets, youth fades, life is an empty dream.

204.   Time will not be ours for ever. (*Ben Jonson*)

205.   The Unknown are better than ill known. (*Abraham Cowley*)

206.   Usually we praise only to be praised. (*La Rochefoucauld*)

207.   The vagabond, when rich, is called a tourist. (*Paul Richard*)

208.   Variety is the soul of pleasure. (*Aphra Benn*)

209.   Victory smiles on those who dare. (*William James Linton*)

210.   Voyaging thro' strange seas of thought, Alone. (*Wordsworth*)

211.   Warbling murmurs of brook. (*Lord Herbert*)

212.   We only part to meet again. (*John Gay*)

213.   We refuse praise from a desire to be praised twice. (*La Rochefoucauld*)

214.   We that live to please must please to live. (*Johnson*)

215.   What a piece of work is man! (*Hamlet*)

216.   What is this life, if full of care. We have no time to stand and stare. (*W. H. Davies*)

217.   When everyone is somebody, then no one's anybody. (*William Schwenck Gilbert*)

218.   When we have shuffled off this mortal coil. (*Hamlet 3 : 1 : 67*)

219.   Whoever lives true life, will love true love. (*E. B. Browning*)

220.   A wilderness of Sweets. (*Paradise Lost 5 : 294*)

221.   Wisdom married to immortal verse. (*Wordsworth*)

222.   Woe came with war and want with woe. (*W. Scott*)

223.   The world is changed with the grandeur of God. (*G. M. Hopkins*)

224.   The world is too much with us. (*Wordsworth*)

225. The world's a prison, no man can get out. (*Berten*)
226. The word Alms has no singular, as if to teach us that a solitary act of charity scarcely deserves the name.
227. Words are but empty thanks. (*Colley Cibber*)
228. X mas is enjoyable, only if it comes once in a year.
229. You shall be more beloving than belov'd. (*Antony & Cleopatra 1 : 2 : 24*)
230. You shall be yet for fairer than you are. (*Antony & Cleopatra 1 : 2 : 18*)
231. Zeal without knowledge is a runaway horse.
232. Zeal fit only for wise men, but is found mostly in fools.
233. Zeal without prudence is frenzy.
234. Let zest and zeal be your pulse and feel.
235. Zeal without knowledge is fire without light.

CHAPTER VIII

Symbols of Animals

1. ant----frugality and prevision
2. ape----uncleanness
3. ass----stupidity
4. bantam cock----pluckiness, priggishness
5. bat----blindness
6. bear----ill-temper, uncouthness
7. bee----industry
8. beetle----blindness
9. bull----strength, straight-forwardness
10. bull-dog----pertinacity
11. butterfly----sportiveness, living in pleasure
12. cat----deceit
13. calf----lumpishness, cowardice
14. cicada----poetry
15. cock----vigilance, overbearing insolence
16. crow----longevity
17. crocodile----hypocrisy
18. cuckoo----cuckoldom
19. dog----fidelity, dirty habits
20. dove----innocence, harmlessness
21. duck----deceit
22. canard (french)----a hoax
23. eagle----majesty, inspiration
24. elephant----sagacity, ponderosity
25. fly----feebleness, insignificance
26. fox----cunning, artifice
27. frog and toad----inspiration
28. goat----lasciviousness
29. goose----conceit, folly
30. gull----gullibility
31. grasshopper----old age
32. hare----timidity

33. hawk----rapacity, penetration
34. hen----maternal care
35. horse----speed, grace
36. jackdaw----vain assumption, empty conceit
37. jay----senseless chatter
38. kitten----playfulness
39. lamb----innocence, sacrifice
40. lark----cheerfulness
41. lion----noble courage
42. lynx----suspicious vigilance
43. magpie----garrulity
44. mole----blindness, obstinacy
45. monkey----tricks
46. mule----obstinacy
47. nightingale----forlornness
48. ostrich----stupidity
49. ox----patience, strength
50. owl----wisdom
51. parrot----mocking verbosity
52. peacock----pride
53. pigeon----cowardice (pigeon-livered)
54. pig----obstinacy, dirtiness
55. puppy----empty-headed conceit
56. rabbit----fecundity
57. raven----ill luck
58. robin red-breast----confiding trust
59. serpent----wisdom
60. sheep----silliness, timidity
61. stag----cuckoldom
62. swallow----a sunshine friend
63. swan----grace
64. swine----filthiness, greed
65. tiger----ferocity/ tortoise----chastity
66. turkey-cock----official insolence
67. turtle-dove----conjugal fidelity
68. vulture----rapine
69. wolf----cruelty, savage ferocity, and rapine
70. worm----cringing

CHAPTER IX

Some Couplets

There are some couplets or distiches which contain two rhyming lines.

Many epigrams are in the form of couplets.

Examples :

When I am dead, I hope it may be said,

His sins were scarlet, but his books were read.

(Hilaire Belloc)

He first deceased, she for a little tried

To live without him, liked it not and died.

(Old Epitaph)

Strange Words : English Examined

Our language is so constituted that it is very easy to make new words or to adapt strange ones, so that there is no art or science which cannot be fully and copiously dealt with in English. But the greatest care ought to be taken, the advice of learned grammarians and the authority of the magistracy (government) should be sought before new or strange words should be admitted into COMMON use: for this childish (shall I say mad?) affection of words is absolutely blameworthy when much more suitable ones could be drawn from our own fount, the affected words obscure the native propriety of the language and make the language itself untrue to its own nature, confused uncertain and burdened with a useless weight of words.

(- Christopher Cooper 1698 from English Examined : Page 54)

Iambic Monometer

Iambic Monometer is a verse in a one-foot line.
There are only a few poems written entirely in iambic monometer.

One such is given below:
    Thus I
    Pass by,
    And die :
    As one
    Unknown
    And gone.
    I'm made
    A shade
    And laid
    I'th' grave :
    These have
    My care
    Where tell
    I dwell
    Farewell.

(-Robert Herrick : Upon His Departure Hence)

CHAPTER X

How Many Senses?

Here are few senses in which English words can be used.

1. In an affirmative sense
2. In a bad sense
3. In a broad sense
4. In a certain sense
5. In a deep sense
6. In a depraved sense
7. In a deteriorated sense
8. In an exclamatory sense
9. In a far deeper sense
10. In a figurative sense
11. In an indirect sense
12. In a large sense of the word
13. In a literal sense
14. In a metaphorical sense
15. In a moral sense
16. In a mystical sense
17. In a negative sense
18. In a narrowly etymological sense
19. In a new sense
20. In a personal sense
21. In a very real sense
22. In a satirical sense
23. In a sense
24. In a special sense
25. In a spiritual sense
26. In a strict sense
27. In a wider sense
28. In a widely different sense
29. In an exaggerated sense
30. In another sense
31. In its broader sense

32. In its metaphorical sense
33. In its medieval sense
34. In its modern sense
35. In its strict sense
36. In its stricter and older sense
37. In its widest sense
38. In one sense
39. In the absolute sense
40. In the academic sense of the term
41. In the classical sense
42. In the direct sense
43. In the ethical sense
44. In the exact sense
45. In the figurative sense
46. In the fullest sense (of the term)
47. In the generally accepted sense (of the term)
48. In the highest sense of the word
49. In the imperative sense
50. In the intimate sense of the term
51. In the logical sense
52. In the main sense
53. In the more narrow sense
54. In the more usual sense of the word
55. In the most pedantical sense of the word
56. In the old sense of the word
57. In the ordinary sense
58. In the original sense of the word
59. In the political sense
60. In the precise and full sense of the word
61. In the proper sense of the word
62. In the purest, least complicated sense of the word
63. In the real sense
64. In the social sense
65. In the strict sense of the word
66. In the superior sense of the word
67. In the true sense of the word
68. In the usual sense
69. In the wider sense/70. In the widest sense of the term

CHAPTER XI

How Many Senses are there in English?

1. Sense of acceptance of life
2. Sense of Accomplishment
3. Sense of achievement
4. Sense of action
5. Sense of actuality
6. Sense of admiration
7. Sense of adventure
8. Sense of the aesthetic
9. Sense of affection
10. Sense of affirmation
11. Sense of Alienation
12. Sense of amoral
13. Sense of anachronism
14. Sense of anticipation
15. Sense of apathy
16. Sense of the appropriate
17. Sense of approval
18. Sense of aridity
19. Sense of artificiality
20. Sense of artistry
21. Sense of atmosphere
22. Sense of authenticity
23. Sense of authority
24. Sense of awe

1. Sense of badness
2. Sense of balance
3. Sense of bearing
4. Sense of beauty
5. Sense of beginning
6. Sense of being alone
7. Sense of betrayed

8. Sense of bewilderment
9. Sense of blessedness
10. Sense of boredom
11. Sense of the business

1. Sense of callousness
2. Sense of carving
3. Sense of change
4. Sense of charm
5. Sense of circumstance
6. Sense of class distinction
7. Sense of coldness
8. Sense of colour
9. Sense of comedy
10. Sense of comfort
11. Sense of communion with the environment
12. Sense of community
13. Sense of community identity
14. Sense of complacency
15. Sense of completeness
16. Sense of completion
17. Sense of compulsion
18. Sense of conflict
19. Sense of confusion
20. Sense of conscience
21. Sense of constraint
22. Sense of contentment
23. Sense of continuity
24. Sense of contrast
25. Sense of the conventional
26. Sense of conviction
27. Sense of coolness
28. Sense of crime
29. Sense of crisis
30. Sense of crusade
31. Sense of cultural diffusion
32. Sense of cunning
33. Sense of curiosity

1. Sense of danger
2. Sense of darkness
3. Sense of death
4. Sense of death and sorrow
5. Sense of decency
6. Sense of decor
7. Sense of decorum
8. Sense of dedication
9. Sense of defeat
10. Sense of defencelessness
11. Sense of degradation
12. Sense of dejection
13. Sense of delicacy
14. Sense of delight
15. Sense of dependence
16. Sense of deprivation
17. Sense of depth
18. Sense of desertion
19. Sense of design
20. Sense of desire
21. Sense of desolation
22. Sense of desperation
23. Sense of destiny
24. Sense of detachment
25. Sense of determinism
26. Sense of development
27. Sense of devotion
28. Sense of dignity
29. Sense of difference(s)
30. Sense of difficulty
31. Sense of dignity
32. Sense of direction
33. Sense of disappointment
34. Sense of discharging one's duty
35. Sense of discipline
36. Sense of disgust
37. Sense of disproportion and unfitness
38. Sense of disquiet

39. Sense of dissatisfaction
40. Sense of distance
41. Sense of divinity
42. Sense of doom
43. Sense of doubt
44. Sense of drama
45. Sense of duration
46. Sense of duty

80. Sense of economy
81. Sense of editorial integrity
82. Sense of egoism
83. Sense of elation
84. Sense of an elemental strength
85. Sense of embarrassment
86. Sense of emptiness
87. Sense of enchantment
88. Sense of ending
89. Sense of enjoyment
90. Sense of enlargement
91. Sense of envy
92. Sense of equality
93. Sense of equity
94. Sense of estrangement
95. Sense of evil
96. Sense of exactitude
97. Sense of excited enjoyment
98. Sense of excitement
99. Sense of exhilaration
100. Sense of expansion
101. Sense of experience
102. Sense of exposure to attacks
103. Sense of extreme uneasiness

104. Sense of failing eyes
105. Sense of failing power in eyes
106. Sense of failing sight
107. Sense of failure

108. Sense of faith
109. Sense of false security
110. Sense of false modesty
111. Sense of false pretence
112. Sense of familiarity
113. Sense of fashion
114. Sense of fate and fatality
115. Sense of fear
116. Sense of filial duty
117. Sense of finality
118. Sense of fine truth
119. Sense of finiteness
120. Sense of fitness
121. Sense of foreboding
122. Sense of form
123. Sense of formality
124. Sense of fragrance
125. Sense of freedom
126. Sense of frustration
127. Sense of fun
128. Sense of fusion
129. Sense of the future
130. Sense of futility

131. Sense of gaiety
132. Sense of gloom
133. Sense of glory
134. Sense of grace
135. Sense of gratitude
136. Sense of greatness
137. Sense of grief
138. Sense of grievance
139. Sense of grotesque incongruity
140. Sense of the grotesque
141. Sense of groundlessness
142. Sense of guilt

143. Sense of happiness

144. Sense of harmony
145. Sense of hearing
146. Sense of helplessness
147. Sense of heritage
148. Sense of high-spirited vivacity
149. Sense of historical accuracy
150. Sense of history
151. Sense of holiness
152. Sense of honesty
153. Sense of honour
154. Sense of hostility
155. Sense of human life
156. Sense of human power
157. Sense of humanity
158. Sense of humility
159. Sense of humour
160. Sense of hurry

161. Sense of identification with the aims of a group
162. Sense of identity
163. Sense of idleness
164. Sense of idiom
165. Sense of ignorance
166. Sense of immediacy
167. Sense of immediate loss
168. Sense of impending disaster
169. Sense of importance
170. Sense of impulse
171. Sense of incompetence
172. Sense of indebtedness
173. Sense of individualism
174. Sense of individuality
175. Sense of inescapability of death
176. Sense of inevitability
177. Sense of inferiority
178. Sense of ingratitude
179. Sense of injured merit
180. Sense of injury

181. Sense of injustice
182. Sense of initiative
183. Sense of insecurity
184. Sense of inspiration
185. Sense of insult
186. Sense of integration
187. Sense of integrity
188. Sense of intellectual effort
189. Sense of intelligent activity
190. Sense of intimacy
191. Sense of intrusion
192. Sense of invention
193. Sense of involvement
194. Sense of irony
195. Sense of irrecoverableness
196. Sense of irresponsibility
197. Sense of isolation

198. Sense of joy
199. Sense of judgment
200. Sense of justice

201. Sense of kinship

202. Sense of labour
203. Sense of leisure
204. Sense of life
205. Sense of loneliness
206. Sense of loss
207. Sense of loss of purpose
208. Sense of loyalty

209. Sense of magnitude
210. Sense of mastery
211. Sense of meaninglessness of life
212. Sense of melody
213. Sense of menace
214. Sense of metamorphosis

215. Sense of metrical properties
216. Sense of military discipline
217. Sense of misery
218. Sense of mission
219. Sense of momentum
220. Sense of moral responsibility
221. Sense of morality
222. Sense of motive
223. Sense of movement
224. Sense of musical delight
225. Sense of mystery
226. Sense of mysticism

227. Sense of national honour
228. Sense of national unity
229. Sense of nationalism
230. Sense of nationality
231. Sense of nationhood
232. Sense of nearness
233. Sense of the necessity for order
234. Sense of nervousness
235. Sense of nobility of the spirit
236. Sense of nostalgia
237. Sense of novelty

238. Sense of obedience
239. Sense of obligation
240. Sense of occasion
241. Sense of oddity
242. Sense of oneness
243. Sense of optimism
244. Sense of order
245. Sense of the original
246. Sense of originality
247. Sense of outrage

248. Sense of pain
249. Sense of paralysis

250. Sense of participation
251. Sense of the passage
252. Sense of the passage of time
253. Sense of the past
254. Sense of pattern
255. Sense of peace
256. Sense of pensiveness
257. Sense of perfection
258. Sense of period
259. Sense of permanence
260. Sense of permanency
261. Sense of personal dignity
262. Sense of personal gallantry
263. Sense of personal identity
264. Sense of personal importance
265. Sense of personal involvement
266. Sense of personal relation
267. Sense of perspective
268. Sense of perversity
269. Sense of physical well being
270. Sense of pity
271. Sense of place
272. Sense of planning
273. Sense of pleasurable relations
274. Sense of pleasure
275. Sense of political competence
276. Sense of political responsibility
277. Sense of pomposity
278. Sense of possession
279. Sense of power
280. Sense of the precarious
281. Sense of presence
282. Sense of principle
283. Sense of piracy
284. Sense of private dignity
285. Sense of professional solidarity
286. Sense of progress
287. Sense of property

288. Sense of proportion
289. Sense of proprietorship
290. Sense of propriety
291. Sense of proximity
292. Sense of prudence
293. Sense of prudery
294. Sense of public duty
295. Sense of purpose

296. Sense of quality

297. Sense of racial superiority
298. Sense of realism
299. Sense of reality
300. Sense of reasoning
301. Sense of regret
302. Sense of relationship
303. Sense of release
304. Sense of relief
305. Sense of religion
306. Sense of remorse
307. Sense of remoteness
308. Sense of renewal
309. Sense of repression
310. Sense of respect
311. Sense of respectability
312. Sense of responsibility
313. Sense of restlessness
314. Sense of restraint
315. Sense of reverence
316. Sense of rhythm
317. Sense of the ridiculous
318. Sense of righteous
319. Sense of righteousness
320. Sense of rightness
321. Sense of romance
322. Sense of ruin

323. Sense of the sacred
324. Sense of sacrifice
325. Sense of sacrilege
326. Sense of sanctuary
327. Sense of seclusion
328. Sense of security
329. Sense of selectivity
330. Sense of self-importance
331. Sense of self-respect
332. Sense of sense
333. Sense of separation
334. Sense of seriousness
335. Sense of shame
336. Sense of shock
337. Sense of sickness
338. Sense of significance
339. Sense of silence
340. Sense of sin
341. Sense of smell
342. Sense of social identity
343. Sense of social justice
344. Sense of social responsibility
345. Sense of social service
346. Sense of society
347. Sense of solemnity
348. Sense of solidarity
349. Sense of spaciousness
350. Sense of spirit of the religion
351. Sense of stability
352. Sense of strain
353. Sense of strangeness
354. Sense of structure
355. Sense of style
356. Sense of sublimity
357. Sense of success
358. Sense of sudden liberation
359. Sense of suffocation
360. Sense of superiority

361. Sense of the supernatural
362. Sense of the supernatural power
363. Sense of surprise
364. Sense of suspicion
365. Sense of symmetry

366. Sense of tact
367. Sense of tension
368. Sense of territory
369. Sense of terror
370. Sense of time
371. Sense of time passing
372. Sense of timelessness
373. Sense of timeliness
374. Sense of touch
375. Sense of tradition
376. Sense of tragedy
377. Sense of tragic fate
378. Sense of tranquillity
379. Sense of triumph
380. Sense of truth

381. Sense of uncertainty
382. Sense of unease
383. Sense of uneasiness
384. Sense of unity
385. Sense of universality
386. Sense of unreality
387. Sense of unworthiness
388. Sense of urgency
389. Sense of uselessness
390. Sense of utter desertion
391. Sense of utter loss

392. Sense of vacuum
393. Sense of the value of time
394. Sense of values
395. Sense of vanity

396. Sense of victory
397. Sense of virtue
398. Sense of vision
399. Sense of vivacity
400. Sense of vocation

401. Sense of weakness
402. Sense of weariness
403. Sense of well being
404. Sense of wonder
405. Sense of worldly dignity
406. Sense of worth
407. Sense of wrong
408. Sense of wrong doing

409. Sense of youth

CHAPTER XII

Strikingly Beautiful Phrases

- The accident of an accident
- We agree to disagree.
- Better than the best
- Best of the best - James Rhoades
- Bitterest bitterness - Francis Thomson
- Breathe the breath - Thomas Hood
- Brutish beasts - Julius Caesar 3 : 2 : 110
- Certain Certainties - T.S. Eliot
- Delicious delicacies
- Descriptive description
- End of the unending
- The endless endlessness of eternity
- Excessive exaggeration
- It is faultily faultless
- To feel a feel of pity for a person
- Gentle gentleman - Arden of Feversham 3 : 1 42
- Ghastly ghost – Swinburne
- Goods of good quality
- Guileless guile - Francis Thomson
- Hallucinatory delusions
- The happiness of the happy - Samuel Rogers
- Hate of hate
- Highest heights
- A homely home - Jerome K. Jerome
- Few men speak humbly of humility, chastely of chastity, skeptically of skepticism – Pascal

- Illogical logic
- Immortal mortal - F. Thompson
- To impede impediments
- Inconceivable conceptions
- Insatiable satiety of sensualism

- You can learn to learn
- Love of loving love
- Make much too much of it
- Misguiding guide
- Momentous moment
- Much of a muchness - Sir John Vanbrough
- A little noiseless noise among the leaves – Keats
- Obscene obscurity
- Perfect perfection
- Pitiable pity – Swinburne
- Poetical poetry
- The purest of the pure – Browning
- To be rarely rare
- To be really real
- Where reason is utterly unreasonable - G.K. Chesterton
- Shadow of a shade
- Shapeless shape
- Unreasonable reason - G.K. Chesterton
- Utterly unutterable rubbish - Swinburne
- Villainous villain
- Voiceless voice
- Womanly woman

CHAPTER XIII

Adverbially Adjective Noun Phrases

Rhythmically Combined Adverbially Adjective Noun Phrases

English is one of the most rhythmical languages of the world. The Dictionary of Alliterative and Rhythmic Phrases contains thousands of rhythmical phrases intermingled with alliterations. Besides such alliteratively rhythmical phrases, there exist in English a large number of adverbially adjective noun phrases (a phrase coined to befit the pattern). Many of such triple - word phrases are presented here for your reference. Such phrases are highly useful for the semantic study of phrase - structures in English.

Absolutely free conscience
Absorbingly interesting occupation
Abundantly illustrated book
Acoustically indistinct consonants
Admittedly difficult task
Apparently disconnected facts
Architecturally successful edifice
Astonishingly young mind
Awfully up-hill work

Badly drawn character
Basically irrelevant detail
Biologically important functions
Bitterly contested wars
Blatantly defied convention
Brightly coloured flowers
Brilliantly written book

Carefully ascertained facts
Carefully chosen examples
Carefully developed theory
Clearly defined pattern
Closely guarded secret
Closely related words

Commercially oriented people
Commonly used words
Comparatively recent development
Completely different angle
Completely illiterate audience
Constantly changing background
Constantly recurring themes
Critically edited text
Currently fashionable dress

Dangerously disparaging attributesDazzlingly beautiful illuminations
Dearly loved person
Deeply felt resentment
Deeply rooted tradition
Delightfully chivalrous statement
Densely populated areas
Divinely inspired poetry

Eagerly awaited news
Easily accomplished task
Economically advanced nation
Economically backward areas
Elegantly dressed person
Eminently readable introduction
Eminently respectable figures
Emotionally charged sound
Entirely unfamiliar country
Exceedingly clever man
Extremely attractive girl
Extremely grave risks
Extremely popular songs

Fairly accurate details
Fairly reliable guide
Fantastically inspiring place
Finely framed speech
Flamboyantly handsome man
Frequently used word

Fully qualified person
Fundamentally different approach

Gaily plumaged birds
Gaudily coloured beaks
Generally accepted fact
Genuinely new ideas
Gorgeously created figures
Grammatically different words
Grievously committed sins

Happily chosen term
Hardly audible sound
Hastily summoned meeting
Heavily bearded person
Highly developed feeling
Highly disciplined community
Highly emotional speeches
Highly readable narrative
Highly sophisticated equipment
Historically correct usage
Historically related family of languages
Honestly earned money
Hugely impressive system

Immensely complicated affairs
Immensely suggestive book
Increasingly inelegant expressions
Increasingly popular subject
Inexpressibly beautiful measure
Infinitely productive artist
Infinitely small quantities
Infinitely variable world
Infinitely varied world
Insipidly pious woman
Intellectually mature person
Intensely interesting experience
Intensely private life

Intensely subjective poet
Internationally known scientist

Juridically free peasants

Keenly analytical ear

Lavishly illustrated pages
Lavishly produced publications
Lawfully constituted authority
Legally wedded wife
Lexicologically interesting polysemy
Linguistically enlightened editors
Literally translated vernacular expressions
Logically coherent analysis
Logically connected sentences
Logically fallacious inferences
Loosely flowing garments

Marvellously engineered road system
Mechanically woven carpet
Mentally disturbed people
Mentally retarded children
Moderately priced book
Mortally wounded man
Mutually exclusive categories
Mutually intelligible dialects

Nationally televised programme
Naturally unstressed words
Neatly furnished house
Negatively charged particle
Negatively prefixed words
Newly appointed minister
Newly constituted board
Newly discovered languages
Newly married man
Newly constructed buildings

Newly published titles
Normally constituted man
Noticeably defective speech
Noticeably handsome face

Objectively verifiable statements
Obviously desirable goal
Officially recognised institutions
Originally distinct words
Originally short form
Originally intended meaning
Outstandingly handsome man
Outstandingly significant feature
Outstandingly intelligent leaders
Outwardly opposing forces

Parochially minded persons
Particularly gifted person
Perfectly acceptable sentences
Perfectly intelligent woman
Perfectly familiar proposition
Perfectly intelligible sentence
Permanently popular work
Phonetically different sounds
Politically oriented socialists
Politically powerful minority groups
Prettily painted room
Previously unpublished reports
Privately printed volume
Profoundly interesting writer
Profoundly religious man
Profusely illustrated book
Properly designed structure
Purely academic journals
Purely imaginative work

Quickly discoverable error

Radically different meaning
Rapidly changing world
Rapidly developing science
Rapidly growing enthusiasm
Really busy person
Really expensive shirt
Recently published novel
Regularly constituted government
Remarkably popular writer
Richly cultured man

Sadistically cruel man
Seemingly contradictory facets (of one's personality)
Seemingly little things
Seemingly worthless people
Semantically peculiar etymology
Semantically (very) interesting words
Singularly fortunate youth
Slightly different meaning
Smartly dressed woman
Socially acceptable qualities
Socially adaptive behaviour
Socially distinct societies
Socially distinguished ladies
Socially useful productive work
Sparsely populated areas
Specially designed building
Specially shaped pipe
Specially written example
Spiritually elevating influence
Spiritually highest realities
Splendidly successful book
Strictly limited interest
Strictly scientific words
Strikingly beautiful places
Strongly developed taste
Strongly marked face
Strongly rooted envy

Strongly worded resolution
Suddenly recollected emotion
Superbly sculptured features
Surprisingly subtle discrimination
Syllogistically expressed agreement
Symbolically significant work
Systematically organised survey

Tacitly accepted values
Thickly populated city
Thinly populated area
Thoroughly dishonest man
Thoroughly learned system
Thoughtfully prepared material
Totally different spirit
Totally unexpected result
Tremendously popular form
Traitorously corrupted youth
Truly good man

Unimaginably beautiful gardens
Uniquely great events
Universally acknowledged truth
Unspeakably bad taste
Utterly different languages
Utterly insignificant person

Vaguely defined term
Vastly increased power
Verbally defined concepts
Vividly attractive pictures

Wholly subjective affair
Widely separated countries
Wildly imaginative mind
Wonderfully rich appearance

CHAPTER XIV

A Medieval Song

Full of Alliterations : The Field Full of Folk

In a somer seson whenne softe was the sunne
I shop me into a shroud as I shep were,
In habite as an hermite unholy of werkes,
Wente wide in this world wondres to here.
But on a May Morwening upon Malverne hilles
Me befel a ferly, or fairye me thoughte.
I was wery of wandred and went me to reste
Under a brod bank by a bournes side.
And as I lay and lenede and lookede on the Watres,
I slomerede into a sleeping, it swyede so merye.

Thenne gan I mete a merveillous swevene:
That I was in a wilderness, wiste I nevere where.
Ac as I beheld into the Est on high to the sunne
I saw a towr on a toft tryely y-maked.
A deep dale benethe, a dungeoun thereinne
With deepe dikes and derke and dredful of sight.
A fair feeld ful of folk fand I there-betwene,
Of alle maner of men, the mene and the riche,
Worching and wandringe as the world asketh.
Some putte hem to plow, playede ful selde,

In setting and sowing swunk ful harde,
Wonne that these wastours with glotonye destroyeth.
And some putte hem ta pride, aparailede hem thereafter,
In countenaunce of ckothing comen disgised.
In prayers and penaunce putten hem manye,
Al for love of oure Lord livede wel straite,
In hope for to have hevene-riche blisse,
As ancres and hermites that holden hem in celles,
Coveite not in cuntre to cairen aboute

For no likerous liflode here likam to plese.

And some chosen to chaffare, they chevede the betere.
As it seemeth to our sight that suche men thriven.
And some merthes to make, as minstrales cunne,
And gete gold with here glee giltles, I trowe.
Ac japeres and jangleres, Judas Children,
Fonden hem fantasies and fooleshem make,
And have wit at wille to worche if hem list.
That Poule percheth of hem I dar not prove it here;
Qui lowuitur turpiloquium is Luciferes hine,
Bidderes and beggeres faste aboute yede

Til here bely and here bagge were bratfuly-crammed;
Flite thenne for her foode, foughten at the ale;
In glotonye, God wot, go they to bedde,
And risen up with ribaudrye as Robertes knaves;
Sleep and sleuthe seweth hem evere,
Pilgrimes and palmeres plighten hem togedere
For to seke Saint Jame and Saintes at Rome;
Wenten forth in here way with many wise tales,
And hadde leve to lye al here lif after.
Hermites on an heep, with hooked staves,

Wenten to walsingham, and here wenches after;
Grete lobies and longe, that loth were to swinke,
Clothe de hem in copes to be knowen from othere,
Shopen hem hermites here ese to have.
I fand there freres, alle all the foure orders,
Preching the peple for profit of the wombe;
Glosede the gospel as hem good likede,
For coveitise of copes construe de it as they wolde.
Many of these maistres may clothe hem at liking.
For here mony and here Marchaundise meten togedere.

Si then charite hath been Chapman chief to shrive lordes.
Manye ferlies han fallen in a fewe yeres.
But Holy church and hy holded bet togedere,

The most michief on molde is mounting up faste.
There prechede a pardoner, as he a preest were,
Brought forthe a bulle with bishopes seeles,
And saide that himself mighte assoile hem alle
Of falsnesse of fasting and of arowes broken.
Lewede men levede it wel and like de his speche,
Comen up kneelinge to kissen his bulle.

He buncheth hem with his brevet and blereth here eye,
And raughte with his raggeman ringes and broches.
Thus they given here gold glotones to helpe
And leneth it loseles that lecherie hauten.
But were the bishop y-blissed and worth bothe his eres.
His seel shulde not be sent to deceive the peple.
It is not al by the bishop that the boy precheth,
Ac the parish preest and the pardoner parte the silver
That the pore peple of the parish shulde have if they ne were.
Persones and parish preeetes plained hem to Gere bishop

That here parish was pore sithe the pestilence time,
To have a licence and leva at Londoun to dwelle,
To singe for simonye- for silver is swete.
There hovede and hundred in houves of silk,
Serjauntes it seemede that serve de at the barre;
Pleten for penies and poundes the lawe,
And nought for love of oure Lord unlose here lippes ones.
Thou mightest bestere mete mist on Malverne hiles.
Thanne gete a mom of here mouth til mony be shewed.
I saw bishopes bolde and ba cheleres of divin,

Become clerkes of a countes the king for to serve,
Archedekenes and denes, that dignites haven
To preche the peple and pore men to feede,
Been y lope to Londoun by leve of here bishop.
And been clerkes of the Kinges Bench the cuntre to shende.
Barouns and burgeis and bondage also.
I saw in that semble, as ye shulen here after.
Baxteres and brocheres and brewsteres manye,

Wollene websteres and weveres of linen,
Taillours and tanneres and tokkeres bothe,

Masones, minours, and manye othere craftes,
As dikeres and delveres that doth here deede ille,
And driveth forth the longe day with

Djeu lave Dame Emme!

Cookes and here knaves crieth 'hote pies, hot!
Goode gees and gris! Go we dine, go we!'
Taverners to hem tolde the same.
'Whit wyn of Osay and wyn of Gascoyne,
Of the Ryn and of the Rochel, the rost to defye!'
AI this I saw sleeping and seven sithes more.

By Willjam Langland c. 1375

CHAPTER XV

Nephelidia : Running Alliterations

From the depth of the dreamy decline of the dawn
    through a notable nimbus of nebulous noonshine,
    Pallid and pink as the palm of the flag-flower that
    flickers with fear of the flies as they float,

Are they looks of our lovers that lustrously lean from a
    marvel of mystic miraculous moonshine,
    These that we feel in the blood of our blushes that
    thicken and threaten with throbs through the throat?

Thicken and thrill as a theatre thronged at appeal of
    actor's appalled agitation
    Fainter with fear of the fires of the future than
    pale with the promise of pride in the pest :

Flushed with the famishing fullness of fever
    that reddens with radiance of rather recreation
    Gaunt as the ghastliest of glimpses that gleam
    through the gloom of the gloaming when ghosts go aghast?

Nay, for the nick of the tick of the time is a
    temulaus touch on the temples of terror,
    Strained as the Sinews yet strenuous with strife
    of the dead who is dumb as the dust-heaps of death :

Surely no soul is it sweet as the spasm of erotic
    emotional exquisite error,
    Bathed in the balms of beautified bliss, beatific
    itself by beatitude's breath.

Surely no spirit or sense of a soul that was soft to
    the spirit and soul of our senses.
    Sweetens the stress of suspiring suspicion that sobc

in the semblance and sound of a sigh :

Only this oracle opens Olympian in mystical moods
    and triangular tenses -
    Life is the lust of a lamp for the light is dark still
    the dawn of the day when we die'.

Mild is the mirk and monotonous musk of memory
    melodiously mute as it may be,
    While the hope in the heart of a hero is bruised by
    the breach of men's rapiers, resigned to the rod :

Made meek as a mother whose bosom-beats bound
    with the bliss-bringing bulk of a balm-breathing baby.
    As they grope through the graveyard of creeds,
    under skies growing green at a groan for the grimness of God.

Blank is the book of his bounty beholden of old,
    and its binding is blacker than bluer :
    Out of blue into black is the scheme of the skies,
    and their dews are the Wine of the bloodshed of things :

Till the darkling desire of delight shall be free as a
    fawn that is freed from the fangs that pursue her.
    Till the hearts of hell shall be hushed by a hymn
    from the hunt that has hurried the kennel of kings.

This Poem (Nephelidia) with running alliterations was written by Algernon Charles Swinburne.

CHAPTER XVI

Hints on Pronunciation for Foreigners

I take it you already know
    of tough and bough and cough and dough?
    Others may stumble, but not you
    on hiccough, thorough, laugh and through?
    Well done! And now you wish perhaps
    to learn of these familiar traps?
    Beware of heard, a dreadful word,
    That looks like beard and sounds like bird,
    And dead: it's said like bed, not bead,
    For Goodness' sake, don't call it deed!
    Watch out for meat and great and threat,
    They rhyme with suite and straight and debt.
    A moth is not a moth in mother.
    Nor broth in brother, broth in brother,
    And here is not a match for there,
    Nor dear and fear, bear and pear,
    And then, ther's does and rose and lose
    Just look them up : and goose and choose,
    And cork and front and word and ward
    And font and front and word and sword.
    And do and go and thwart and cart -
    Come, come, I've hardly made a start!
    A dreadful language? Man alive,
    I'd mastered it when I was five!
Anonymous

CHAPTER XVII

Singular Singulars and Peculiar Plurals...

How singular some old words are!
   I know two with no singular.
   Agenda and marginalia : Both
   Are always plural, 'pon my oath.
   The opposite's the case to greet us
   With propaganda and coitus,
   Upon these never sets the sun,
   And yet of each there's only one.
   Phantasmagoria, likewise,
   Pervades, yet never multiplies.
   Strata pluralises stratum,
   Ultimata and ultimatum.
   Memoranda and memorandum
   Candelabra and candelabrum.
   Why are nostrums then not nostra?
   Why speak I not then from rostra?
   Thus my datum grows to data,
   My erratum to errata.
   Child, put this on your next agendum.
   Pudenda's more than are pudendum
   Medium makes media.
   Criterion, criteria.
   What's plural for hysteria?

CHAPTER XVIII

What is the plural?

No one for spelling at a loss is
   Who boldly spells Rhinocerosses.
   I've known a few (I can't say lots)
   Who called the beasts Rhinocerots.
   Though they are not so bad (O fie!)
   As those who pay Rhinoceri.
   One I have heard (O holy Moses)
   Who plainly said Rhinoceroses.
   While possibly a Fourth-Form Boy
   Might venture on Rhinoceroi
   The moral that I draw from these is
   The plural's what one damn well pleases.
Anonymous

CHAPTER XIX

Plurals

We'll begin with a box, and the plural is boxes,
But the plural of ox becomes oxen, not oxes.
One fowl is a goose, but two are called geese,
Yet the plural of moose should never be meese.

You may find a lone mouse or a nest full of mice,
Yet the plural of house is houses, not hice,
    And if Father is Pop, how come Mother's not Mop?
    If the plural of man is always called men,
Why shouldn't the plural of pan be called pen?
If I speak of my foot and show you my feet,
And I give you a boot, would a pair be called beet?
    If one is a tooth and a whole set are teeth,
Why shouldn't the plural of booth be called beeth?
    We speak of a brother and also of brethren,
But though we say mother, we never say methren.
    Then the masculine pronouns are he, his and him,
But imagine the feminine: she, shis and shim!
    Let's face it – English is a crazy language.
There is no egg in eggplant nor ham in hamburger; neither apple nor pine in
pineapple.
English muffins weren't invented in England or French fries in France.
    We take English for granted, but if we explore its paradoxes,
We find that quicksand can work slowly, boxing rings are square,
    And a guinea pig is neither from Guinea nor is it a pig.
    And why is it that writers write but fingers don't fing,
    Grocers don't groce and hammers don't ham?
    Doesn't it seem crazy that you can make amends but not one amend.
    If teachers taught, why didn't preachers praught?
If a vegetarian eats vegetables, what does a humanitarian eat?
    In what other language do people recite at a play and play at a recital?
We ship by truck but send cargo by ship.
We have noses that run and feet that smell.

We park in a driveway and drive in a parkway.
And how can a slim chance and a fat chance be the same?
    You have to marvel at the unique lunacy of a language
in which your house can burn up as it burns down,
in which you fill in a form by filling it out, and
in which an alarm goes off by going on.
    And in closing, when I wind up my watch, I start it, but when I wind up this poem, I end it?

CHAPTER XX

A gentle echo on women

In the Doric manner
Shepherd :
Echo, I ween, will in the word reply,
And quaintly answer questions :
Shall I try?
Echo : Try
What must we do our passion to express?
Press
How shall I please her, who ne'er loved before?
Be Fore.
What most moves women when we them dress?
A Dress.
Say, what can keep her chaste whom I adore?
A door.
If music softens rocks, love tunes my lyre.
Liar.
Then teach me echo, how shall I come by her?
Buy Her.
When bought, no question I shall be her dear?
Her Deer.
But dear have horns: how must I keep her under?
Keep her under.
But what can glad me when she's laid in bier?
Beer.
What must I do when women will be kind?
Be Kind.
What must I do when women will be cross?
Be Cross.
Lord, what is she that can so turn and wind?
Wind.
If she be wind, what stills her when she blows?
Blows.
But if she bang again, still should I bang her?

Bang Her.
Is there no way to moderate her anger?
Hang Her.
Thanks, gentle Echo! Right thy answer tell
What woman is and how to guard her well.
Guard her Well.
By Jonathan Swift

Why English is so hard?

We'll begin with a box and the plural is boxes.
But the plural of ox should be oxen, not axes.

Then one fowl is goose, but two are called geese.
Yet the plural of moose should never be meese.

You may find a lone mouse or a whole lot of mice.
But the plural of house is houses, not hice.

If the plural of man is always called men,
Why shouldn't the plural of pan be called pen?

The cow in the plural may be cows or kine.
But the plural of vow is vows, not vine.

And I speak of a foot and you show me your feet.
But I give you a boot - would a pair be called beet?

If one is a tooth and the whole set are teeth.
Why shouldn't the plural of booth be called beeth?

If the singular is this and the plural is these,
Should the plural of kiss be nicknamed kese?

Then one may be that and three may be those,
Yet the plural of hat would never be hose.

We speak of a brother and also of brethren,

But though we say mother, we never say mothren.

The masculine pronouns are he, his, and him,
But imagine the feminine she, shis and shim!

The Process of Conception

Beneath those parts, where stretching to its bound,
The low Abdomen grids the Belly round,
The Shop of nature lies, a vacant Space,
Of small Circumference divides the Place,
Pear-like the Shape : within a Membrane spreads,
Her various texture of meandrous Threds.
These draw the vessels to a pursy State,
And or contract their substance, or dilate,
Here veins, Nerves, Arteries in pairs declare,
How robler parts deserve a double Care.
They form the mass the Blood and Spirits drain,
That irrigate profuse the thirsty Plain.
The Bottom of the Womb 'tis call'd. The Sides are cleft,
By Cells distinguish'd into Right and Left,
'Tis thought that Females in the Left prevail,
And that the Right contains the sprightly Male,
A passage here in Form oblong extends,
Where fast compress'd the stiffen'd Nerve ascends,
And the warm Fluid with concurring Fluids blends.
The Sages this the Womb's neck justly name.
Within the hollow of its inward Frame,
Join'd to the parts a small protuberance grows,
Whose rising hips the deep Recesses close.
For while the Tiller all his strength collects,
While Hope anticipates the fair Effects,
The lubricated parts their Station leave,
And closely to the working Engine cleave.
Each Vessel stretches, and distending wide,
The greedy Womb attracts in glowing Tide,
And either Sex Commix'd, the Streams united glide,
But now the Womb relax'd, with pleasing pair

Gently subsides into itself again.
The Seed moves with it, and thus clos'd within,
The tender Drops of Entity begin,
What Joy the Fibres of the stomach feel.
Long pinch'd with Hunger, at a greatful Meal,
Such tickling pleasure throu the Womb is Sent,
When the first particles of Life ferment,
This easy picture of the Parts explains,
How frequent Motion no Effect obtains.
The Seed and Pleasure lost in eager Strife;
A useful Lesson to the forward Wife.

From Callipaedia or the Art of Getting Beautiful Children (Book II) :
Translated from Latin by George Sewell : 1688-1726

The Praise of English

The Italian is pleasant but without sinews, as too stilly fleeting water : The French delicate but overnice, as a woman scarce daring to open her lips for fear of marring her countenance : the Spanish majestical but fulsome, running too much on the o, and terrible like the devil in a play : the Dutch manlike, but withal very harsh, as one ready at every word to pick a quarrel. Now we in borrowing from them give the strength of consonants to the Italian, the full sound of words to the French, the variety of terminations to the Spanish and the mollifying of more vowels to the Dutch : and so, like bees, gather the honey of their good properties and leave the dregs to themselves. And thus, when substantialness combineth with delightfulness with fineness, seemliness with portliness and courrantness with staidness, how can the language which consisteth of all these sound other than most full of sweetness?

Again, the long words that we borrow, being intermingled with the short of our own store, make up a perfect harmony, by culling from out which mixture (with judgement) you may frame your speech according to the matter you must work on, majestical pleasant, delicate or manly, more or less, in what sort of you please. Add here unto, that whatsoever grace any other language carrieth, in verse or prose, in tropes or metaphors, in echoes or agnominations, they may all be lively and exactly represented in ours.

Will you have Plato's vein?

Read Sir Thomas Smith : the Ionic?

Sir Thomas Moore : Ciceros?

Ascham : Varro? Chaucer : Demosthenes? Sir John Cheke (who in his Treatise to the Rebels hath comprised all the figures of rhetoric).

Will you read Virgil?

Take the Earl of Surrey : Catullus? Shakespeare and Marlow's fragment : Ovid? Daniel : Lucan? Spenser : Martial? Sir John Davis and others.

Will you have all in all for prose and verse?

Take the miracle of our age, Sir Philip Sidney.

By Richard Carew : 1555-1620 : An Epistle on the Excellency of the English Tongue

CHAPTER XXI

Tongue-Twisters

It is suggested that tongue-twisters should be used by the students to practise our tongue to make the pronunciation clear and perfect.

Do not memorize all the tongue twisters. That will only confuse you. Memorize one twister and try to repeat it at least twenty times non-stop.

Betty Botter bought some butter but she said my batter's bitter. If I buy some better butter it will make my batter better. So she bought some better butter and it made her batter better. (*This Tongue-twister was sent to us by our friend Lesley from Ottery St Mary, Devon, UK.*)

1. A good cook could cook as much cookies as a good cook who could cook cookies.

1. I saw a saw that could out saw any other saw I ever saw.

3. Black bug bit a big black bear. But where is the big black bear that the big black bug bit?

4. A big bug bit the little beetle but the little beetle bit the big bug back.

5. I thought, I thought of thinking of thanking you.

6. RED BULB BLUE BULB RED BULB BLUE BULB RED BLOOD BLUE BLOOD.

7. I wish to wish the wish you wish to wish, but if you wish the wish the witch wishes, I won't wish the wish you wish to wish.

8. If a sledering snail went down a slippery slide would a snail sleder or slide down the slide.

9. These thousand tricky tongue twisters trip thrillingly off the tongue .

10. Sounding by sound is a sound method of sounding sounds.

11. Lala Gope Gappungam Das.

12. You curse, I curse, we all curse, for asparagus!

13. Kacha papaya pacca papaya Kacha papaya pacca papaya Kacha papaya pacca papaya.

14. Sanjeev's sixth sheep is sick.

15. Double bubble gum, bubbles double.

16. Betty bought butter but the butter was bitter, so Betty bought better butter to make the bitter butter better.

17. A sailor went to sea to see, what he could see. And all he could see Was sea, sea, sea.

18. A box of mixed biscuits, a mixed biscuit box.

19. Upper roller lower roller Upper roller lower roller.

20. Purple Paper People, Purple Paper People, Purple Paper People.

21. If two witches were watching two watches, which witch would watch which watch?

22. SIXTH SICK SHEIK'S SIXTH SICK SHEEP.

23. Which watch did which witch wear and which witch wore which watch?

24. Six slippery snails, slid slowly seaward.

25. How much wood could a wood chuck; chuck if a wood chuck could chuck wood.

26. I scream, you scream, we all scream for ice cream!

27. Paresh P Patel plans to peel potatoes in Pune.

28. An Ape hates grape cakes.

29. She sells sea shells on the sea shore she sells sea shells no more.

30. I slit a sheet, a sheet I slit. And on a slitted sheet I sit. I slit a sheet, a sheet I slit. The sheet I slit, that sheet was it.

31. Any noise annoys an oyster but a noisy noise annoys an oyster more.

32. Do tongue twisters twist your tongue?

33. How much wood could a wood chopper chop, if a wood chopper could chop wood?

34. If a black bug bleeds black blood, what color blood does a blue bug bleed?

35. Pooped purple pelicans.

36. Betty block brought some bric a brac.

37. Cuthbert's cuff links.

38. Tie a knot, tie a knot.

Tie a tight, tight knot.
Tie a knot in the shape of a nought.

39. If two witches were watching two watches, which witch would watch which watch?

40. Sounding by sound is a sound method of sounding sounds.

41. I wish to wish the wish you wish to wish, but if you wish the wish the witch wishes, I won't wish the wish you wish to wish.

42. I thought a thought. But the thought I thought wasn't the thought I thought I thought. If the thought I thought I thought had been the thought I thought, I wouldn't have thought so much.

43. Fresh fried fish, Fish fresh fried, Fried fish fresh, Fish fried fresh.

44. Red Leather, Yellow Leather.

Red Leather, Yellow Leather.
Red Leather, Yellow Leather.

45. Betty Botter bought some butter, but she said "this butter's bitter! But a bit of better butter will but make my butter better" So she bought some better butter, better than the bitter butter, and it made her butter better so 'twas better Betty Botter bought a bit of better butter!

46. A Tudor who tooted a flute
Tried to tutor two tooters to toot.
Said the two to their tutor,
Is it harder to toot;
Or to tutor two tooters to toot.

47. A flea and a fly flew up in a flue.
Said the flea, "Let us fly!"
Said the fly, "Let us flee!"
So they flew through a flaw in the flue.

48. Yellow butter, purple jelly, red jam, black bread.
Spread it thick, say it quick!
Yellow butter, purple jelly, red jam, black bread.
Spread it thicker, say it quicker!
Yellow butter, purple jelly, red jam, black bread.
Don't eat with your mouth full!

CHAPTER XXII

Portmanteau Words

Portmanteau Words are the one that blend the sounds and the meanings of two words. The word **Portmanteau** is derived from the *French* word *portmanteau*, combined from *porter* (to carry) and *manteau*(mantle). While these Words originated in 16th century, Lewis Carroll is credited with coining this word (in Through the Looking Glass) based on the fact that portmanteau bag is one that opens into two equal parts.

However, many such Words catch on and latch on to the lexicon. Others do not and simply fade away into silent sunsets, having enjoyed their 15 minutes of glory.

The meanings of all such words are apparent from the combination. Most of these words will not be found in standard dictionaries. But, the visitors can use their grey cells in putting the meanings of the two and two together to deduce the meaning of these words.

Portmanteau Words are also called <u>Centaur Words</u>. Absatively = absolutely + positively (This word was sent to us by our friend **Celeste** from USA.)

1. Adflation = advertising + inflation
2. Beautility = beauty + utility
3. Bit = binary + digit
4. Bitini = bitsy + bikini
5. Blog = web + log
6. Bonk = bang + conk
7. Breathalyzer = breath + analyzer
8. Brunch = breakfast + lunch
9. Camcorder = camera + recorder
10. Chortle = chuckle + snort
11. Cremains = cremated + remains
11. Chunnel= channel + tunnel
12. Diplonomics=diplomacy + economics
13. E-commerce = electronic + commerce
14. Email= electronic + mail
15. Faction= fact + fiction

16. Fantabulous= fantastic+ fabulous
17. Fanzine= fanatic + magazine
18. Feminar= feminine + seminar
19. Frarority= fraternity + sorority
20. Gasohol= gasoline + alcohol
21. Ginormous= gigantic + enormous
22. Guestimate= guess + estimate
23. Hi-tech= high + technology
24. Heliport + helicopter + airport
25. Internet = international + network
26. Interpol- international + police
27. Jackpot= jack + pot
28. Jaywalk= jay + walk
29. Jerkwater = jerk + water
30. Joypad= joystick + pad
31. Laundromat = laundry + automat
32. Manimal = man + animal
33. Medevac = medical + evacuation
34. Medicare = medical + care
35. Mobike= motor + bike
36. Modem = MOdulator + DEModulator
37. Moped= motor + pedal
38. Motel= motor + hotel
39. Motorcade= motorcar + cavalcade
40. Netiquette = Internet + etiquette
41. Netizen = Internet + citizen
42. Newscast = news + broadcast
43. Oxbridge = Oxford + Cambridge
44. Paratroop = parachute + troop
45. Permalink = permanent + link
46. Pluot = plum + apricot
47. Podcast = iPod + broadcasting
48. Sci-Fi= science + fiction
49. Sexploitation = sex + exploitation
50. Sexcercise = sex + exercise
51. Sexting = Sex + texting
52. Shamateur= sham+ amateur
53. Smog = smoke + fog

54. Splurge= splash+ surge
55. Telecast= television + broadcast
56. Telethon = telephone (or television) + marathon
57. Telecom = telephone + Communication(s)
58. Televangelist= television + evangelist
59. Toughicult = tough + difficult
60. Transistor= transfer + resistor
61. Vash= volcanic + ash
62. Webinar = web + seminar
63. Workfar= work + welfare

CHAPTER XXIII

Man of Many Kinds

1. Man of ability
2. Man of absolute genius
3. Man of absolute honesty
4. Man of absolutely fastidious tastes
5. Man of account
6. Man of achievement
7. Man of action
8. Man of active and resilient mind
9. Man of active habits
10. Man of acute hearing
11. Man of adamantine honesty
12. Man of affairs
13. Man of affluence
14. Man of all work
15. Man of ardent temperament
16. Man of ardent political convictions
17. Man of artistic sensibility
18. Man of authority
19. Man of blood
20. Man of breeding
21. Man of brick
22. Man of brilliant genius
23. Man of boundless energy
24. Man of business
25. Man of candour
26. Man of capacity
27. Man of character
28. Man of charming personality
29. Man of clear understanding
30. Man of clerical responsibilities
31. Man of cold temperament
32. Man of colour

33. Man of a commanding presence
34. Man of commanding appearance
35. Man of commanding genius
36. Man of common birth
37. Man of common sense
38. Man of compelling personality
39. Man of compromise
40. Man of conscience
41. Man of considerable attainments
42. Man of considerable learning
43. Man of considerable taste
44. Man of considerable wealth
45. Man of consummate prudence
46. Man of contention
47. Man of conviction
48. Man of courage
49. Man of courtly nurture
50. Man of critical temper
51. Man of cultivation
52. Man of culture
53. Man of culture and experience
54. Man of decision
55. Man of deeds
56. Man of destiny
57. Man of devotion
58. Man of different calibre
59. Man of dignified bearing
60. Man of discriminating taste
61. Man of distinction
62. Man of distinguished abilities
63. Man of distinguished intelligence
64. Man of education
65. Man of eminence
66. Man of eminently noble character
67. Man of energetic action
68. Man of energy
69. Man of erudition
70. Man of evil repute

71. Man of exact mind
72. Man of exalted genius
73. Man of very exceptional mind and sensibility
74. Man of excessive sensibility
75. Man of extraordinary qualities
76. Man of extraordinary sensibility
77. Man of extremes
78. Man of fancy
79. Man of family
80. Man of fashion
81. Man of fertile and ingenious mind
82. Man of few words
83. Man of the field
84. Man of fiery temperament
85. Man of fine conversation
86. Man of the first rank
87. Man of flesh and blood
88. Man of force
89. Man of fortune
90. Man of fulfilled loves
91. Man of the future
92. Man of genius Man of god
93. Man of good heart
94. Man of good repute
95. Man of good sense
96. Man of goodly personage
97. Man of great ability
98. Man of great charm
99. Man of great conversational powers
100. Man of great courage
101. Man of great distinction
102. Man of great erudition
103. Man of great esteem
104. Man of great gravity
105. Man of great heart
106. Man of great independence of mind
107. Man of great integrity
108. Man of great merit

109. Man of great moral courage
110. Man of great quality
111. Man of great wealth
112. Man of great zeal
113. Man of guile
114. Man of handsome property
115. Man of hard work and few words
116. Man of high ability
117. Man of high character
118. Man of high distinction
119. Man of high extraction
120. Man of High principles
121. Man of high rank
122. Man of the highest eminence in political history
123. Man of his word
124. Man of honour
125. Man of honour and glory
126. Man of the hour
127. Man of humble birth
128. Man of humble origin
129. Man of ill judgement
130. Man of imagination
131. Man of imaginative genius
132. Man of imbalanced habits
133. Man of imperturbable temperament
134. Man of importance
135. Man of incorruptible integrity
136. Man of independent means
137. Man of independent mind
138. Man of inferior ability
139. Man of inferior birth
140. Man of influence
141. Man of integrity
142. Man of intellect
143. Man of intellectual integrity
144. Man of intelligence
145. Man of inward light
146. Man of iron

147. Man of iron determination
148. Man of iron will
149. Man of judgement
150. Man of justice
151. Man of knowledge
152. Man of labour
153. Man of law
154. Man of learning
155. Man of learning and judgement
156. Man of legendary strength
157. Man of leisure
158. Man of letters
159. Man of literary genius
160. Man of literary habits
161. Man of literary interests
162. Man of literary power
163. Man of literature
164. Man of little imagination
165. Man of little information
166. Man of many accomplishments
167. Man of many acquisitions
168. Man of many excellent qualities
169. Man of many faults
170. Man of many interests
171. Man of many parts
172. Man of many resources
173. Man of many trades
174. Man of many wiles
175. Man of many words
176. Man of mark
177. Man of marked excellence
178. Man of marvellous energy
179. Man of maturity
180. Man of maturity and wisdom
181. Man of mean birth
182. Man of mean understanding
183. Man of means
184. Man of mediocrity

185. Man of medium height
186. Man of memories
187. Man of merit
188. Man of mettle
189. Man of middle size
190. Man of middling height
191. Man of mighty name
192. Man of mild disposition
193. Man of moderate birth
194. Man of moderate fortune
195. Man of modest means
196. Man of money
197. Man of moods
198. Man of morality
199. Man of morals
200. Man of musical sensibility
201. Man of nasty ideas
202. Man of negative view point
203. Man of negotiation
204. Man of noble birth
205. Man of note
206. Man of optimism
207. Man of ordinary intelligence
208. Man of outstanding ability
209. Man of outstanding genius
210. Man of paradoxes
211. Man of parts
212. Man of peace
213. Man of the people
214. Man of personal popularity
215. Man of piety
216. Man of pleasure
217. Man of polite learning
218. Man of political power
219. Man of position
220. Man of power
221. Man of powerful mind
222. Man of practical wisdom

223. Man of practically no ideas
224. Man of the press
225. Man of principle
226. Man of private virtue
227. Man of prodigious endurance
228. Man of prominence
229. Man of property
230. Man of prudence
231. Man of public virtue
232. Man of pure mind
233. Man of purpose
234. Man of quality
235. Man of rank
236. Man of rare attainments
237. Man of real sensibility
238. Man of refined manners
239. Man of refined taste
240. Man of religion
241. Man of remarkable energy
242. Man of remarkable gifts
243. Man of remarkable quality
244. Man of renown
245. Man of respectable appearance
246. Man of respectable talents
247. Man of rigid morals
248. Man of ripe experience
249. Man of romantic tradition
250. Man of saintly life
251. Man of science
252. Man of self-respect
253. Man of sense
254. Man of sensibility
255. Man of sensitive culture
256. Man of sensitive nature
257. Man of simplicity of soul
258. Man of singular merit
259. Man of singularly delicate constitution
260. Man of singularly sincere character

261. Man of skilful hand
262. Man of small stature
263. Man of social standing
264. Man of social worth
265. Man of some abilities
266. Man of some account
267. Man of some background
268. Man of some scientific reputation
269. Man of some social standing
270. Man of some substance
271. Man of sorrows
272. Man of sound judgement
273. Man of the soundest judgement
274. Man of sovereign parts
275. Man of spirit
276. Man of splendid abilities
277. Man of spotless life
278. Man of standing
279. Man of stature
280. Man of stern and stubborn principles
281. Man of straw
282. Man of strict principles
283. Man of strife
284. Man of strong action
285. Man of strong build
286. Man of strong character
287. Man of strong common sense
288. Man of strong intellect
289. Man of strong mind
290. Man of strong passions
291. Man of strong physique
292. Man of strong sense
293. Man of strong views
294. Man of strong will and decided character
295. Man of stubbornness
296. Man of substance
297. Man of subtle reasoning
298. Man of superior abilities

299. Man of superior education
300. Man of swarthy appearance
301. Man of sweet manners
302. Man of talent
303. Man of taste
304. Man of the theatre
305. Man of thought
306. Man of true genius
307. Man of two-fold character
308. Man of unblemished character
309. Man of uncertain temper
310. Man of unclear lips
311. Man of understanding
312. Man of unlimited resource
313. Man of valour
314. Man of varied attainments
315. Man of various information
316. Man of vast information
317. Man of vast minds
318. Man of very high reputation Man of violent passions
319. Man of virtue
320. Man of vision
321. Man of war
322. Man of weak nerves
323. Man of wealth
324. Man of wealth and importance
325. Man of wide culture
326. Man of wide interests
327. Man of wide reading
328. Man of wit
329. Man of words
330. Man of worth
331. Man of zeal

CHAPTER XXIV

A Proverbial Conversation

As Love and I late harbour'd in one inn,

With proverbs thus each other entestain :

"In love there is no back': thus I begin :

"Fair words make fools," replieth he again :

"Who spares to speak doth spare to speed," quoth I :

"As well," said he, "too forward as too slow" :

"Fortune assists the boldest," I reply :

"A hasty man," quoth he, "ne'er wanted woe":

"Labour is light where I love", quoth I, "doth pay":

Saith he, "Light burden's heavy, if farborne":

Quoth I, The main lost. Cast the by away":

"Y' have spun a fair thread", he replies in scorn.

And having thus a while each other thwarted

Fools as we met, so fools again we parted.

By Michael Drayton : Proverbs

CHAPTER XXV

Wealth of Vocabulary

How Many ways are There?

Airway,Archway,Anyway,Away
   Broadway
   Cableway,Crossway,Cutaway
   Doorway
   Entryway,Everyway
   Gateway,Guideway
   Halfway,Hallway,Hatchway,Headway
   Leeway
   Midway,Milkyway
   Outway
   Passageway,Proper way,Pathway
   Railway,Roadway,Runway
   Seaway,Shipway,Someway,Stairway,Straightaway
   Tramway
   Walkway,Waterway

Count The Days

Alackaday / Birthday / Christmas day / Doomsday / Easter day / Everyday / Friday / Holiday / Judgement day / Lord's Day / Market day / Midday / Monday / Noonday / Pay day / Quarter day / Saturday / Sunday / Today / Tuesday / Thursday / Wednesday / Wedding day / Weekday / Workday / Working day / Yesterday

Ocracies : -cracy

Here is the list of words ending in -cracy.
   Androcracy/Aristocracy/Arithmocracy/Autocracy
   Bureaucracy
   Chrysocracy/Cosmocracy/Cottonocracy

Democracy/Demonocracy/Despotocracy/Doulocracy
Echoencephalocracy/Ergatocracy/Ethnocracy
Gernotocracy/Gerontocracy/Gynaecocracy
Hagiocracy/Hierocracy/Hypocracy
Idiocracy/Isocracy
Landocracy/Logocracy
Kleptocracy
Millionocracy/Mobocracy/Monocracy
Neocracy/Nomocracy
Ochlocracy
Pantisocracy/Pedantocracy/Physhocracy/Plantocracy/Plousiocracy/
Plutocracy/Ptochocracy
Shopocracy/Slavocracy/Snobocracy/Stratocracy
Technocracy/Thallassocracy/Theocracy/Timocracy

Ographies : -graphy

This list provides the Words (Ographies) ending in -graphy.
Amniography/Anthography/Anthropography
Archaeography/Autobiography/Autography
Balneography/Bibliography/Bioautography/Biography
Cacography/Calcography/Caledography/Calligraphy
Cardiography/Cartography/Cerography/Chalcography
Chartography/Chirography/Chomolithography
Chorography/Christianography/Chromatography
Chromophotography/Chromotypography/Chromoxylography
Chronography/Cinematography/Climatography
Cochromatography/Cometography/Cosmography
Cryptography/Crystallography/Dactyliography
Demography/Dendrography
Ecclesiography/Electroretinography
Epigraphy/Epistolography
Ethnography/Ethography/Galvanography
Geography/Glossography/Glyphography
Glyptography/Gypsography
Hagiography/Haliography/Haplography/Heliography
Heliotypography/Hematography/Heresiography
Heterography/Hetersiography/Hierography

Histography/Historiography/Holography
Homography/Horography/Horologiography
Hyalography/Hydrography/Hyetography
Hymnography/Hypsography/Ichnography
Ichthyography/Iconography
Ideography/Isography
Lexicography/Lexigraphy/Lichenography
Lipography/Lithography/Logography
Macrograph/Mammography/Mechanography
Mediography/Metallography/Micrography
Microcosmography/Mimography/Monography
Morphography/Myography/Mythography
Neography/Neurography/Nomography
Nosography/Numismatography
Oceanography/Odontography/Ontography
Ophiography/Oreography/Organography
Orography/Orthography/Osteography
Palaeontography/Paneiconography
Pantography/Papyrography/Perspectography
Petrography/Phamacography/Photography
Phantasmatography/Phonography
Phycography/Physiography/Phytography
Planography/Plastography/Pneumatography
Pneumography/Poligraphy/Pornography
Potamography/Psalmography/Pseudepigraphy
Pseudography/Psychobiography/Psychography
Pterylography/Pyrography/Pythogeography
Radiography/Reprography/Rhyparography
Salenography/Scenography/Sciography
Scotography/Seismography/Sematography
Semeiography/Siderography/Sigillography
Skeletography/Sphenography/Stegnagraphy
Stelography/Stenography/Stereography
Stereotypography/Stratigraphy/Stratography
Stylography/Symbolaeography
Tacheography/Technography/Thalassography
Thanatography/Thermography/Topography
Toreumatography/Typography

Uranography
Xylography/Zenography/Zincography
Zoogeography/Zoography/Zylopyrography

phobia

This **ROOT-WORD** is **PHOBIA** which comes from Greek word Phobos which means **IRRATIONAL FEAR**.There are innumerable words with this suffix PHOBIA. The list is endless. Here a collection of few words with this suffix-PHOBIA has been given.

The fequesntly used Phobias

1.Achluophobia : Irrational fear of dark places
2.Acoustic phobia: Irrational fear of sounds
3.Acrophobia : Irrational fear of heights
4.Aerophobia : Irrational fear of aero planes or flying or air
5.Agoraphobia : Irrational fear of open space
6.Ailurophobia : Irrational fear of cats
7.Algophobia : Irrational fear of pain
8.Androphobia : Irrational fear of men
9.Anemophobia : Irrational fear of wind
10.Apiophobia : Irrational fear of bees
11.Aqua phobia : Irrational fear of water
12.Arachnophobia : Irrational fear of spiders
13.Archnophobia : Irrational fear of spiders
14.Asthenophobia : Irrational fear of weakness
15.Astrophobia : Irrational fear of lightning
16.Auto phobia : Irrational fear of loneliness
17.Basiphobia : Irrational fear of walking
18.Bathophobia : Irrational fear of depths or deep places
19.Belonophobia : Irrational fear of needles
20.Botanophobia : Irrational fear of plants
21.Brontophobia : Irrational fear of thunder
22.Cacophobia : Irrational fear of ugliness
23.Callophobia : Irrational fear of beauty
24.Cheimophobia : Irrational fear of cold
25.Chionophobia : Irrational fear of snow
26.Chromo phobia: Irrational fear of colors
27.Chronophobia : Irrational fear of time

28.Claustrophobia : Irrational fear of confined places
29.Climacophobia : Irrational fear of stairs
30.Coitophobia : Irrational fear of sexual intercourse
31.Coprophobia : Irrational fear of faces
32.Cremiophobia : Irrational fear of loneliness
33.Cremonophobia: Irrational fear of heights
34.Cryophobia : Irrational fear of cold
35.Cynophobia : Irrational fear of dogs
36.Demo phobia : Irrational fear of people
37.Dermatophobia : Irrational fear of skin
38.Dipsophobia : Irrational fear of drinking or drunkenness
39.Dora phobia : Irrational fear of fur
40.Dromophobia : Irrational fear of streets or crossing streets
41.Emetophobia : Irrational fear of vomiting
42.Entomophobia : Irrational fear of insects
43.Eragsiophobia : Irrational fear of surgery
44.Eremiophobia : Irrational fear of stillness
45.Ergophobia : Irrational fear of work
46.Erythrophobia : Irrational fear of red
47.Galeophobia : Irrational fear of sharks
48.Gatophobia : Irrational fear of cats
49.Genophobia : Irrational fear of birth
50.Gephyrophobia : Irrational fear of bridges
51.Geraphobia : Irrational fear of old age
52.Gerascophobia : Irrational fear of old age
53.Gerontophobia : Irrational fear of old man
54.Geumophobia : Irrational fear of taste
55.Glossophobia : Irrational fear of public-speaking
56.Graphophobia : Irrational fear of writing
57.Gymnophobia : Irrational fear of nakedness
58.Gynaephobia : Irrational fear of women
59.Gynophobia : Irrational fear of marriage
60.Haematophobia: Irrational fear of blood
61.Haemophobia : Irrational fear of blood
62.Harpaxophobia : Irrational fear of robbers
63.Hedonophobia : Irrational fear of pleasure
64.Heliophobia : Irrational fear of Sunlight
65.Helminthophobia: Irrational fear of worms

66.Hippo phobia : Irrational fear of horses
67.Hodophobia : Irrational fear of travel
68.Homophobia : Irrational fear of sameness
69.Hydrophobia : Irrational fear of water
70.Hypnophobia : Irrational fear of sleep
71.Hypsophobia : Irrational fear of heights
72.Iatrophobia : Irrational fear of doctors
73.Ichthyophobia : Irrational fear of fish
74.Iophobia : Irrational fear of poisoning
75.Keno phobia : Irrational fear of going out in public or emptiness
76.Keraunophobia : Irrational fear of lightning and thunder
77.Kleptophobia : Irrational fear of thieves
78.Lalophobia : Irrational fear of speaking
79.Logo phobia : Irrational fear of words
80.Lygophobia : Irrational fear of dark places
81.Lyssophobia : Irrational fear of madness
82.Maieusiophobia: Irrational fear of childbirth
83.Mania phobia : Irrational fear of madness
84.Mastrophobia : Irrational fear of breasts
85.Melissophobia : Irrational fear of bees
86.Micro phobia : Irrational fear of small things
87.Microbiophobia: Irrational fear of germs
88.Mono phobia : Irrational fear of solitude
89.Musophobia : Irrational fear of mice
90.Necrophobia : Irrational fear of death or dead bodies
91.Neophobia : Irrational fear of newness
92.Nosophobis : Irrational fear of illness
93.Nyctophobia : Irrational fear of dark places
94.Nyctophobia : Irrational fear of nights
95.Ochlophobia : Irrational fear of crowds
96.Odontophobia : Irrational fear of teeth
97.Odynophobia : Irrational fear of pain
98.Ombrophobia : Irrational fear of rain
99.Onomatophobia: Irrational fear of a particular word
100..Ophidiophobia : Irrational fear of snakes
101.Ophidiophobia: Irrational fear of snakes
102.Ophthalmophobia: Irrational fear of eyes
103.Ornithophobia : Irrational fear of birds

104.Osmophobia: Irrational fear of odors
105.Paedophobia : Irrational fear of children
106.Pantophobia : Irrational fear of everything
107.Pathophobia : Irrational fear of illness
108.Peccatophobia: Irrational fear of sinning
109.Peniophobia: Irrational fear of penury
110.Phasmophobia : Irrational fear of ghosts
111.Phemophobia: Irrational fear of voices
112.Phobophobia : Irrational fear of fear
113.Phonophobia : Irrational fear of sound
114.Phronemophobia: Irrational fear of thinking
115.Plutophopbia: Irrational fear of wealth
116.Pnigeropphobia: Irrational fear smothering
117.Pnigophobia : Irrational fear of choking
118.Podophobia : Irrational fear of feet
119.Poinophobia : Irrational fear of punishments
120.Pornophobia : Irrational fear of Prostitutes
121.Potamophobia : Irrational fear of rivers
122.Psychrophobia : Irrational fear of cold
123.Pterophobia : Irrational fear of aero planes or flying
124.Pyrophobia : Irrational fear of fire
125.Scelerophobia : Irrational fear of burglars
126.Scoileciphobia : Irrational fear of worms
127.Scoptophobia : Irrational fear of watching
128.Scotophobia : Irrational fear of dark places
129.Siderodromophobia: Irrational fear of trains
130.Siderophobia : Irrational fear of stars
131.Sthenophobia : Irrational fear of strength
132.Synophobia : Irrational fear of togetherness
133.Taco phobia : Irrational fear of speed
134.Taeniophobia : Irrational fear of tapeworms
135.Taphophobia : Irrational fear of burial alive
136.Thalassophobia: Irrational fear of oceans
137.Thanatophobia : Irrational fear of death or dead bodies
138.Thermo phobia : Irrational fear of heat
139.Tomophobia : Irrational fear of surgery
140.Tonitrophobia : Irrational fear of thunder
141.Topophobia : Irrational fear of particular place

142.Toxicophobia : Irrational fear of poisoning
143.Traumatophobia: Irrational fear of injury
144.Triskaidekaphobia: Irrational fear of the number thirteen
145.Xenophobia : Irrational fear of foreigners
146.Xerophobia : Irrational fear of deserts or dry places
147.Zoophobia : Irrational fear of animals

Other Phobias

1.   Aerophobia : Irrational fear of aero planes or flying
1.   Pterophobia : Irrational fear of aero planes or flying
3.   Zoophobia : Irrational fear of animals
4.   Apiophobia : Irrational fear of bees
5.   Melissophobia : Irrational fear of bees
6.   Ornithophobia : Irrational fear of birds
7.   Haemophobia : Irrational fear of blood
8.   Haematophobia : Irrational fear of blood
9.   Gephyrophobia : Irrational fear of bridges
10. Taphophobia : Irrational fear of burial alive
11. Ailurophobia : Irrational fear of cats
12. Gatophobia : Irrational fear of cats
13. Pacdophobia : Irrational fear of children
14. Pnigophobia : Irrational fear of choking
15. Psychrophobia : Irrational fear of cold
16. Cheimophobia : Irrational fear of cold
17. Cyrophobia : Irrational fear of cold
18. Claustrophobia : Irrational fear of confined places
19. Demo phobia : Irrational fear of confined places
20. Scotophobia : Irrational fear of dark places
21. Nyctophobia : Irrational fear of dark places
22. Achluophobia : Irrational fear of dark places
23. Lygophobia : Irrational fear of dark places
24. Necrophobia : Irrational fear of death or dead bodies
25. Thanatophobia : Irrational fear of death or dead bodies
26. Bathophobia : Irrational fear of depths or deep places
27. Xerophobia : Irrational fear of deserts or dry places
28. Cynophobia : Irrational fear of dogs
29. Dipsophobia : Irrational fear of drinking or drunkenness

30. Phobophobia : Irrational fear of fear
31. Pyrophobia : Irrational fear of fire
32. Ichthyophobia : Irrational fear of fish
33. Xenophobia : Irrational fear of foreigners
34. Dora phobia : Irrational fear of fur
35. Microbiophobia : Irrational fear of germs
36. Phasmophobia : Irrational fear of ghosts
37. Thermo phobia : Irrational fear of heat
38. Acrophobia : Irrational fear of heights
39. Hypsophobia : Irrational fear of heights
40. Cremonophobia : Irrational fear of heights
41. Hippo phobia : Irrational fear of horses
42. Nosophobis : Irrational fear of illness
43. Pathophobia : Irrational fear of illness
44. Traumatophobia : Irrational fear of injury
45. Entomophobia : Irrational fear of insects
46. Astrapophobia : Irrational fear of lightning
47. Keraunophobia : Irrational fear of lightning
48. Monophobia : Irrational fear of loneliness
49. Auto phobia : Irrational fear of loneliness
50. Cremiophobia : Irrational fear of loneliness
51. Mania phobia : Irrational fear of madness
52. Lyssophobia : Irrational fear of madness
53. Androphobia : Irrational fear of men
54. Musophobia : Irrational fear of mice
55. Onomatophobia : Irrational fear of a particular word
56. Phonophobia : Irrational fear of sound
57. Gerascophobia : Irrational fear of old age
58. Agoraphobia : Irrational fear of open space
59. Keno phobia : Irrational fear of going out in public
60. Topophobia : Irrational fear of particular place
61. Toxicophobia : Irrational fear of poisoning
62. Iophobia : Irrational fear of poisoning
63. Maleusiophobia : Irrational fear of pregnancy
64. Thalassophobia : Irrational fear of sea
65. Galeophobia : Irrational fear of sharks
66. Hypnophobia : Irrational fear of sleep
67. Ophidiophobia : Irrational fear of snakes

68. Lalophobia : Irrational fear of speaking
69. Glossophobia : Irrational fear of public-speaking
70. Taco phobia : Irrational fear of speed
71. Archnophobia : Irrational fear of spiders
72. Dromophobia : Irrational fear of streets or crossing streets
73. Eragsiophobia : Irrational fear of surgery
74. Tomophobia : Irrational fear of surgery
75. Triskaidekaphobia: Irrational fear of the number thirteen
76. Keraunophobia : Irrational fear of thunder
77. Brontophobia : Irrational fear of thunder
78. Tonitrophobia : Irrational fear of thunder
79. Siderodromophobia: Irrational fear of trains
80. Hodophobia : Irrational fear of travel
81. Hydrophobia : Irrational fear of water
82. Aqua phobia : Irrational fear of water
83. Hygrophobia : Irrational fear of water
84. Gynophobia : Irrational fear of water
85. Helminthophobia : Irrational fear of worms
86. Scoileciphobia : Irrational fear of worms
87. Hippopotomonstrosesquippedaliophobia is the fear of long words
88. Didaskaleinophobia is the fear of going to school
89. Phobatrivaphobia is a fear of trivia about phobias

Meters in English

Here is the list of words (Meters) ending in -meter.
accelerometer/acidimeter/actinometer
aerometer/alkalimeter/altimeter/audiometer
ammeter/anemometer/atmometer
barometer/bolometer
calorimeter/ceilometer/centimeter
chronometer/clinometer/colorimeter
coulometer/cyclometer
decameter/decimeter/dekameter
densitometer/diameter/diffractometer
dilatometer/dimeter/dosimeter
durometer/dynamometer

electrodynamometer/electrometer

ergometer/eudiometer/extensometer

flowmeter/fluorimeter/fluorometer

galvanometer/gasometer/geometer

goniometer/gradiometer/gravimeter

hectometer/heliometer/hemacytometer

hemocytometer/heptameter/hexameter

hydrometer/hygrometer/hypermeter

Hypsometer

interferometer/intervalometer/Inclinometer

kilometer/Kiolmeter

Lactometer/Leptometer/Limeter

Logometer/Lucimeter

lysimeter

Macrometer/Magnetometer/Manometer

Meter/Microcalorimeter/Microdensitometer

Micrometer/Microphotometer

Microspectrophotometer/Millimeter

Monometer/Multiparameter

Nanometer/Nauropometer

Nephelometer/Nitrometer

Octameter/Odometer/Ohmmeter

Oleometer/Olfactometer/Ombrometer

Oncometer/Ondometer/Oometer

Opsimeter/Optometer/Orometer

Oscillometer/Osmometer/Ozonometer

Pantometer/Parameter/Passometer

Pedometer/Pelvimeter/Penetrometer

Pentameter/Perimeter/Phonometer

Photometer/Photopolarimeter

Piezometer/Planimeter/Planometer

Platometer/Pluriometer/Pneumatometer

Polarimeter/Potentiometer/Potometer

Psychometer/Psychrometer/Pulmometer

Pulsimeter/Pulsometer/Pycnometer

Pyrheliometer/Pyrometer

Radiometer/Reflectometer/Refractometer

Rehometer/Respirometer/Ratemeter

Rheometer/Rhysimeter/Rotameter
Saccharimeter/Saccharometer/Salilmeter
Salinometer/Salometer/Scimeter
Scintillometer/Sclerometer/Seismometer
Semidiameter/Sensitometer/Sepometer
Silometer/Sonometer/Sphygmomanometer
Spirometer/Spectrofluorimeter/Spirometer
Spectrometer/Spectrophotometer/Stactometer
Speedometer/Spherometer/Sphygmanometer
Sterometer/Stethometer/Stratometer
Stylometer/Submillimeter
Tacheometer/Tachometer/Tannometer
Tasimeter/Taximeter/Telemeter
Tellurometer/Tenderometer/Tensiometer
Tetrameter/Thallasometer/Thanatometer
Thermometer/Tiltmeter/Tonometer
Transmissometer/Tribometer/Trimeter
Trochometer/Tronometer
Tropometer/Turbidimeter
Udometer/Urinometer
Variometer/Velocimeter/Vibrometer
Viscometer/Viscosimeter/Voltmeter
Volumenometer/Volumeter
Wattmeter/Yawmeter
Zymometer/Zymosimeter

Ologies : -logy

Here is the list of words (Ologies) ending in -logy.
Abiology/Accrinology/Acidology/Actinology
Acyrology/Aerology/Aetiology/Agathology
Agmatology/Agriobiology/Agriology/Agrology
Agrostology/Algology/Ambrology/Amphibiology
Amphiology/Anemology/Angelology/Antapology
Anthology/Anthropology/Aphnology/Apology
Arachnology/Archeology/Areology/Aristology
Arthrology/Asthenology/Astrobiology/Astrogeology
Astrology/Atheology/Atomology/Auxology/Axiology

Bacteriology/Barology/Battology/Biaspeleology
Bibliology/Biology/Bryology
Caliology/Campanology/Carcinology/Cardiology
Carpology/Cartology/Cetology/Chirology
Chorology/Chresmology/Christology/Chronology
Chrysology/Climatology/Combinatorial Topology
Conchology/Conchyliology/Cosmology/Craniology
Criminology/Cryobiology/Cryptology/Cynology
Crytomorphology/Cytoecology/Cytology
Dactyliology/Dactylology/Demonology/Dendrology
Deontology/Dermatology/Desmology/Diabology
Dialectology/Dicaeology/Dittology
Dosology/Doxology/Docimology
Ecclesiology/Ecology/Ecophysiology
Edaphology/Egyptology/Electro-biology
Electrology/Electro-physiology/Emblemotology
Embryology/Emetology/Emmenology/Endemiology
Enteradenology/Entomology/Entozoology/Ergology
Epidemiology/Epistemology/Erotology/Eschatology
Esthetology/Ethnology/Ethology/Etiology
Etymology/Exobiology/Exocrinology/Fetology
Filicology/Fossilology/Fungology/Futurology
Galvanology/Gastrology/Gemmology/Genesiology
Geology/Geomorphology/Geratology/Giantology
Glossology/Glottology/Gnomology/Gnosiology
Graphiology/Gynaecology/Gypsology
Haematology/Hagiology/Hamartiology
Haplology/Heliology/Heortology/Heresiology
Heterology/Hibernology/Hierology/Hippology
Histology/Historiology/Homology/Horology
Hydrology/Hyetology/Hygiology/Hygrology
Hylology/Hymenology/Hymnology
Hypnology/Hysterology
Iatrology/Ichnolithnology/Ichnology/Ichorology
Ichthyology/Iconology/Ideology/Idiopsychology
Immunohistology/Immunology/Immunopathology
Kinology/Koniology/Kymatology
Laryngology/Latrology/Lexicology/Lichenology

Limnology/Lithology/Liturgiology
Machanology/Macrology/Malacology/Mantology
Martyrology/Mastology/Mateology/Maternology
Mazology/Melittology/Membranology/Menology
Metamorphology/Meteorology/Methodology
Miasmology/Microbiology/Microgeology
Micrology/Misology/Mommiology/Monadology
Monology/Morphology/Muscology/Mycology
Myology/Mythology
Necrology/Neology/Neontology/Nephrology
Neuralogy/Neurobiology/Neuroendocrinology
Neuropathology/Neuropharmacology/Numismatology
Neurypnology/Nomology/Noology/Nosology
Oceanology/Odology/Odontology/Oenology
Olfactology/Ology/Ombrology/Oneirology
Onology/Onomatology/Ontology/Oology/Ovology
Opiology/Opthamology/Orchidology/Organology
Orismology/Ornithichnology/Orology/Orthology
Osmonosology/Osteology/Otology/Ourology
Palaeophytology/Palaeopsyshology/Palaeothenology
Palaeozoology/Palaetiology/Paleology/Pantheology
Pantology/Papyrology/Paradoxology/Paramology
Parasitology/Parisology/Paromiology/Parthenology
Pathology/Patobiology/Patrology/Patronomatology
Pedology/Pekinglogy/Penology/Periodology
Perissology/Petrology/Phenology/Philematology
Phlebology/Phonology/Photology/Phraseology
Phrenology/Phycology/Physiology/Phytolithology
Phytology/Phytopathology/Phyto-physiology
Piscotology/Planetology/Plutology/Pneumatology
Pneumology/Podology/Pogonology/Pomology
Ponerology/Posology/Potamalogy/Praxiology
Promology/Protophytology/Pseudology/Psilology
Psychology/Psychonosology/Psychopathology
Pteridology/Pterology/Ptochology/Punnology
Pyretology/Pyritology/Pyrology
Quinology
Radiology/Rhematology/Rheology/Runology

Sarcology/Seismology/Selenology/Semantology
Semeiology/Sexology/Sinology/Sitology
Skeletology/Sociology/Somatology/Sophiology
Soteriology/Spasmology/Speciology/Spectrology
Speleology/Spermatology/Sphygmology
Splenology/Splanchnology/Statistology
Stomatology/Stromatology/Symbology/Systematology
Symptomatology/Synchronology/Syndesmology
Tautology/Taxology/Technology/Teleology
Terminology/Termonology/Testaceology
Tetratology/Thanatology/Thaumatology
Thematology/Theology/Theomythology
Thereology/Thermology/Therology
Thremmatology/Threpsology/Tidology
Timbrology/Tocology/Tonology/Topology
Toreumatology/Toxicology/Trichology
Tropology/Typology
Universology/Uranology/Urology
Uronology/Utology
Vexillology/Victimology/Vulcanology
Xenobiology
Zoology/Zoophytology/Zylology/Zymology

mania

This **ROOT-WORD** is the suffix **MANIA** which comes from Greek word
mania which means **ADDICTION TO & EXCESSIVE OBSSESSION WITH** .
This ROOT is used only as a suffix.There are innumerable words with this
suffix. Here a collection of few words has been given.

1. Dipsomania : Addiction to alcohol
1. Bibliomania : Addiction to books
3. Gephyromania : Addiction to crossing bridges
4. Ailuromania : Addiction to cats
5. Demo mania : Addiction to being in the crowd
6. Ochlomania : Addiction to being in the crowd
7. Necromania : Addiction to being with dead-bodies
8. Thanatomania : Addiction to experiencing death

9.   Cynomania : Addiction to being in the dogs
10.   Narcomania : Addiction to drugs
11.   Phagomania : Addiction to excessive eating
12.   Sitomania : Addiction to excessive eating
13.   Phyromania : Addiction to raising fire
14.   Pyromania : Addiction to being amidst fire.
15.   Anthomania : Addiction to flowers
16.   Hippomania : Addiction to horses
17.   Mythomania : Addiction to lying or exaggerating
18.   Egomania : Addiction to talking about oneself
19.   Abhulutomania : Addiction to personal cleanliness
20.   Megalomania : Addiction to exercising one's power
21.   Hedonpmania : Addiction to excessive pleasure
22.   Theo mania : Addiction to religious studies
23.   Entheomania : Addiction to religious studies
24.   Pluto mania : Addiction to being rich
25.   Chrematomania : Addiction to being rich
26.   Erotomania : Addiction to excessive sex
27.   Nymphomania : Addiction to excessive sex
28.   Satyromania : Addiction to excessive sex
29.   Monomania : Addiction to one idea or thing
30.   Kleptomania : Addiction to stealing
31.   Tomomania : Addiction to surgery or undergoing surgery
32.   Logomania : Addiction to talking & talking
33.   Verbomania : Addiction to talking & talking
34.   Dromomania : Addiction to traveling
35.   Hodomania : Addiction to traveling
36.   Porimania : Addiction to traveling

Time for everything

There is a time for everything. To everything there is a season and a time to every purpose under the heaven.

A time to be born and a time to die : A time to plant and a time to pluck up & that which is planted.

A time to kill and a time to heal : a time to break down and a time to build up.

A time to weep and a time to laugh : a time to mourn and a time to dance.

A time to cast away stones and a time to gather stones together : a time to embrace and a time to refrain from embracing.

A time to get and a time to lose : a time to keep and a time to cast away.

A time to rend and a time to sew : a time to keep silence and a time to speak.

A time to love and a time to hate : a time of war and a time of peace.

Triplets or Three Line Stanzas

The dawn was apple green.

The sky was green wine held up in the sun.

The moon was a golden petal between.

She opened her eyes and green.

They shone, clear, like flowers undone

For the first time, now for the last time seen.

By D. H. Lawrence

What are those ravens doing inner trees?

Calling on doom and outworn prophecies?

Flying in trees.........

By Louis Untermeyer

Whoe' er she be,

That not impossible she,

That shall command my heart and me.

By Richard Crashaw

CHAPTER XXVI

Beauties of English Language

The beauty of the English language is in its suppleness and rich variety of words and the vast source of its words. There are words from so many languages; Viking words, Roman words, Anglo-Saxon words, French words, Celtic words, American words, and more. It is a Western Germanic language and yet to my mind, it has a softer and more fluid structure and sound than German, being influenced by so many languages. It is a great language to have fun with, due to its suppleness and absolutely huge and constantly globally influenced and growing vocabulary. For me the ultimate beauty, is how I have been able to play with this language like no other, ever since I first heard it and started to speak it as a baby! I have learnt several other languages, including French, Italian and Russian, and Welsh: and for me, English will always be my favourite, ooops! well! I can play with it most of all, and it is not because my vocabulary is greater in English, it is immediately easier to play with: it has less rigid, traditional, fixed structures to stick to. It also has a directness to it, which suits my personality and it is not inclined to be fancy and fussy, which I respect and find very beautiful.

****

Oh Nishu please don't kiss me on lips at all...!!
Oh Nishu please don't kiss me on lips at...!!
Oh Nishu please don't kiss me on lips...!!
Oh Nishu please don't kiss me on...!!
Oh Nishu please don't kiss me...!!
Oh Nishu please don't kiss...!!
Oh Nishu please don't...!!
Oh Nishu please...!!
Oh Nishu...!!
Oh...!!
O...!!

Here I noticed that when I removed one words from the sentence, this also leads to a beautiful story.

****

"Why I Love the English Language" by Emma Bates

English, despite not being the most-spoken language in the world by some margin, has become an almost universally accepted lingua franca, and the language of choice for students to learn if they want to get ahead in life.

Yet most of the reasons for this don't have very much to do with what a wonderful language it is. It's the language of business and finance, mostly thanks to the economic dominance of Britain in the 19th century and the USA in the 20th. It's the predominant language of film and music, but with lyrics like, 'All I wanted was to break your walls/ All you ever did was wreck me' appearing in number 1 slots worldwide, it's hard to claim that the linguistic beauty of the English language is responsible. The endurance of the myth that English only beat German by a single vote to become the official language of the USA sums up the general attitude to the English language; it has gained global popularity by chance, not by merit.

Knowing how the English language works is like seeing the complex mechanism behind a clock.

All the same, it is a wonderful language. Anyone who has ever studied Wilfred Owen, made their own dress or studied cinematography (bear with me here) will understand the loveliness of things that, when examined and dissected, don't lose their charm but in fact gain something in the greater understanding, like opening up the back of a pocket watch to see the intricate mechanism inside. That's what the English language is like; that's one of the many reasons it's so worth studying. What's on the surface is pretty enough, but dive in and you'll see that there's so much more going on underneath.

Synonyms galore

It's a cliché, and an inaccurate one at that, to say that English has more words than any other language. Certainly, English has a lot of words, and a friend of mine once won a case of champagne betting that it had more words than German. What's lovely about English, though, is that its huge lexical richness follows certain deeply satisfying patterns. Unlike other European languages that are essentially just variations on Latin – which does, admittedly, give them an aural prettiness that English could be said to be lacking – English has had multiple waves of influences that makes it something of a mongrel tongue. And as dog breeders know, mongrels may not be the prettiest, but they are certainly hardier than their purebred relatives. Unlike other languages, where a loanword often entirely replaces its predecessor (does anyone in France still say 'fin de semaine'?) English has a habit of adding extra words, until the language is suffused with synonyms.

Kingly, royal or regal?

Better still, it does so in a particularly elegant way, relating to the three (ish) main sources of words. Anglo-Saxon words are still, in the main, read as simple, easy to understand, or even crude. French words are somewhat more sophisticated. Those who'd like others to know about their level of education but can't quite bring themselves to wear their degree classification on a t-shirt will favour words derived from Latin. Occasionally and delightfully, these three sources will each provide one word for the same thing, as occurs with 'kingly' (as said by the peasant), 'royal' (as said by the courtier) and 'regal' (as said by the scholar). Eight hundred years ago, each of these people would be speaking a different language; now, they use a different vocabulary that nonetheless maps on to almost exactly the same social distinctions. English history is encoded on the English language, and though it doesn't say much for social mobility, there's still something pleasing in how it plays out in the language today.

The tendency of the English language to borrow aggressively from other languages didn't stop with the Norman invasion. Renaissance scholars added the bulk of the Latin and Greek words in use today, and the expansion of British trade and the British Empire led to a hugely varied assortment of words joining the language in subsequent centuries, so that we now have splendid-sounding words like kiosk, kayak and kangaroo seasoning the broth as well.

'Hedgehog' sounds like an Anglo-Saxon compound, but in fact appeared relatively late in Middle English.

One result of having so much vocabulary with so many origins is that English is utterly fantastic for puns. An American lecturer of mine once referred to Terry Pratchett "sharing the English delusion that puns are funny"; perhaps this 'delusion' exists simply because English is such a versatile and fun language in which to pun. Get four English speakers in a pub, make a comment about fish and see what happens – one of them will be "floundering", another "cod do batter" and a third will be "feeling koi" and not join in. Suggest cheese and they won't be able to "camembert it" and the whole cycle will start over again. From the cringe-worthy examples above to the elegant winner of the 2009 Edinburgh Fringe's funniest joke – "why can't hedgehogs just share?" – the sheer range of homophones and near-homophones in English makes wordplay a delight. There's a certain irreverence to all of this; despite its primary modern use as the language of business, English is at heart a language to have fun with.

A truly democratic language?

The main reason it's impossible to say that English has more words than any other language is that no one knows exactly how many words it actually has. We can count the number of words in various major dictionaries easily enough, but no dictionary is definitive. Where other languages have regulators, like the Académie française or the Rat für deutsche Rechtschreibung, English has no such thing. No central body. No one to fix dubious spelling patterns, arbitrate on the acceptability of the singular "they" or defend the subjunctive – but no one, either, to bar new and useful loanwords from entering the language, or to prevent English from evolving organically, according to the needs of English speakers. There is no body of Dumbledoresque old men to control where the language goes and how it should be spoken – and if anyone tried to institute one, it seems likely that the vast majority of the world's 1.5 billion English speakers would ignore its pronouncements anyway.

Anyone can influence the English language; no one can dictate its direction.

The consequence of this is that English is more-or-less democratic. Change to the language happens by consensus, not by decree. And yes, it does mean that we're stuck with ridiculousness like "i before e except after c" (and also just about every other letter in the alphabet), but it also means that as an English speaker, I have just about as much influence over the direction of the language as you do, or as the Merton Professors of English in Oxford do, or even, potentially, as someone who is only just learning their first few words of English does. The only effective way to influence the language is to be good at using it – and that's why Shakespeare gets the credit for inventing 1,700 English words. If not truly democratic, English is certainly more meritocratic than many other languages in the world.

This is all the more worthy of note because any time anyone has succeeded in forcing 'improvements' on the English language in an authoritarian, imposed sort of way, it's almost always made things worse. Think about the utterly unnecessary introduction of the letter 'b' into words like 'debt' and 'doubt', not added to give English teachers extra words to add on spelling tests (though it may seem that way) but in order to give the English words a closer resemblance to their Latin roots. The desire to make English resemble Latin – a language with which it does not have all that much in common grammatically – also gives us the commandment not to split infinitives, which, if obeyed, would have ruined the opening of Star Trek. Like Einstein's comment on genius – "if you judge a fish by its ability to climb a tree, it will live its whole life believing that it is stupid" – English has often suffered for not being Latin.

Oscar Wilde wrote that, "we have everything in common with America nowadays, except, of course, language."

Another dismal failure of English language intervention is Noah Webster's spelling reforms. Some have been readily accepted (we no longer listen to musick), some never caught on (we don't suffer a headake) but the most confusing are the middle ground of changes, accepted on one side of the Atlantic but not the other. So we're stuck with traveler and traveller,color and colour, center and centre, a source of annoyance for editors everywhere.

This resistance of English to central control is not just one of the reasons it's such a widely-spoken language today; it's also central to its development. Received wisdom holds that the clearly Germanic language of Old English evolved into the hybrid Middle English as a result of the Norman invasion and the resulting influence of Norman French. That is certainly true, but it's also only half of the story. The three-part division in the language that I spoke about earlier – the peasantry speaking English, the nobility speaking French and the intelligentsia speaking Latin – came about at this time, superceding Anglo-Saxon efforts to make the use of English universal among the different social classes.

English poetry underwent a revival in the 14th century.

That meant that what had previously been a language spoken, written and taught by the most educated in society as well as the least educated was then handed over almost entirely to the peasantry. English didn't re-emerge as a language that could acceptably be used by people of status at least until the Alliterative Revival of the 14th century, and arguably until Chaucer (for which he earns the title of 'The Father of English Literature'). For around 300 years it was free from interference by the sorts of people who would seek to preserve its more archaic and clunky structures, and therefore evolved naturally. I adore Old English, but it's a language that's full of redundancies and unnecessary grammatical complication, such as a strict case system and relatively strict rules on word order – one or the other will do; you don't need both. Those 300 years of French influence and intellectual neglect stripped English of most of its case system and most of its grammatical gender, as well as simplifying verb endings and making many strong verbs weak, a process that continues to this day. Like antibiotic-resistant bacteria, a challenge to the English language that could have resulted in its annihilation instead just made it stronger.

It's arguable that something similar is happening to English today. The majority of conversations in English happen without a native speaker present; the rise of ELF (English as a Lingua Franca) means that use of English internationally is increasingly about finding the most expedient method of communication rather than any concern about linguistic showiness. English is still shedding redundancies: the subjunctive really only survives in fossilised forms like 'God save the Queen', the possessive apostrophe is looking sickly and some experts are predicting that the third person singular '-s' verb ending (e.g. she runs) could be on the way out too. This is where the lack of a centralised authority is vital to survival. Current English speakers may cringe at the thought of saying "he study hard" or similar, but English speakers 400 years ago would probably have mourned the loss of 'thee' and 'thou', an egalitarian change to the language that most English speakers nowadays appreciate. Trying to hold back the organic evolution of language is reminiscent of a primordial fish clinging to the nascent stub of a tetrapod's foot and saying, "you know, it's a bad idea to go up on land..." What's great about English is that for most of its history, such attempts have failed.

The most beautiful language in the world

'Butterfly' derives from the Old English 'buttorfleoge'; the idea that the word was once 'flutterby' is a myth.

There's a joke that goes like this: there's an English speaker, a French speaker, a Spanish speaker and a German speaker, and they're having a conversation about language. "English is beautiful," the English speaker sighs. "Listen to this: butterfly!" The French speaker nods and says, "yes, French is beautiful too: papillon!" The Spanish speaker smiles and says, "and Spanish as well: mariposa!" The German speaker huffs and frowns, and eventually says, "look, what is your problem with Schmetterling?"

I mention this joke not because it's particularly funny (unless you're telling it in a large group with several Germans, in which case it's hilarious), but because it's one of the few instances I can think of where English is grouped with the 'beautiful' languages instead of the 'ugly' ones. It's an accepted truth that French is better for romance and Italian is better for music. It isn't just a Germanic/Romance distinction, though: Icelandic is very pretty. English seldom gets this kind of praise, and the accents that make it sound more euphonious often do so because they're picking up the rhythms and inflection of a different language and applying it to English, as with Irish pronunciations of words like 'thirty' and 'film'.

Like the iconic Ikea bookcase, English is what you make of it.

I think that's OK. Many languages that sound beautiful do so because of their consistency – Icelandic, for instance, hasn't changed all that much in a thousand years, whereas one of the key elements that makes English so wonderful is, as I've discussed, its sheer mongrel variety. English doesn't have the beauty of a Chippendale wardrobe; it's more the linguistic equivalent of an Ikea Billy bookcase. It's not superficially attractive, but it's also accessible to pretty much anyone, and there are no restrictions on what you do with it once you've got it. Versatile, rich and democratic, the nature of English allows any speaker to express themselves more or less any way they want – and if that isn't beautiful, I don't know what is.

****

Here are some words which are little bit unique.

1.Ardor = passion

2. Asterism = a group of star

3. Wayfarer = someone who travels, especially on foot

4. Eximious = excellent

5.Demure = reserved and shy

6. Uppity = self important, arrogant

7. Opulence = great wealth luxuriousness

8. Yatta = the state of joy after you accomplish a task

9. Woot = to express happiness usually over the internet

10. Kalon = beauty that is more then skin deep

11. Paroxysms = sudden outburst of emotions

12. Salshi = plethoras of love ...

CHAPTER XXVII

Paradox

A paradox is a statement, which appears to be true and false at the same time. A paradoxical statement Is self-contradicting, that defies logic and common sense, and still possibly true. It takes you a while to get a grip on such statements, even though it stares right at you. Here are some interesting samples.

1. 'I always lie' is one of the classic paradox examples because if I always lie, then I would be lying now too. If we are considering the above untrue, then it implies that I don't always lie, which mean if this statement is in fact true, then it's probably false.
2. This is the beginning of the end.
3. Mozambique is a rich country of poor people.
4. Please ignore the notice.
5. Advertisement: If you are illiterate, then write to us and we will send you a free of charge instruction booklet on how to read.
6. I can resist anything except temptation.
7. I know that I know nothing." Knowing "know nothing" is knowing something thus cannot be "know nothing". This statement is self-contradictory, but one does find out that they know nothing.
8. Nobody goes to that restaurant, it's too crowded.
9. Don't go near water until you've learned to swim.
10. If you get this message, call me; if you don't, then don't worry about it.
11. In a country where a ruthless king ruled, there were stringent rules and regulation including the rule which banned the villagers from hunting on the King's premises. Anyone who violated rules was to be condemned to death. When the courtiers, approached the King in this matter, he softened and decreed that the culprit can decide whether he wants to die through beheading or hanging. One clever tramp rescued himself from this fate by requesting that if his statement is true, he should be beheaded but if it is false, he should be hanged. His statement was "I shall be hanged". This baffled the King and the court as they did not know if they hang him, rendering his statement true, that means he ought to be hanged and thus breaking the law. If he was to be beheaded, making his

statement false, then he should be hanged. Paradox never gets solved and the poacher goes free.

12. *"If you wish to preserve your secret, wrap it up in frankness. "* ~ Alexander Smith

The first time you read the sentence given above, you'll probably pass it off, as a joke of some sort, because secrets are meant to be hidden, by the very meaning of the word. But on reading it again, you'll realize, that it does make sense. How often have we seen that things hidden in plain sight, are the least likely to be spotted easily. Once we know that something is a secret, it is human nature, to think that it must be concealed in a place where no one can find it. We never look at the most obvious place, because we believe that it cannot be 'hidden' there. The sentence given above means exactly that, thus making it one of the good literary examples of paradox.

CHAPTER XXVIII

Origin of Idioms

Ever wondered where some frequently used idioms in the English language originated from? Here are some fascinating and sometimes bizarre history of some of the most commonly used sayings.

1. "Pull someone's leg"

Definition: Joking or fooling with someone.

Origin: To pull someone's leg had much more sinister overtones when it first came in use. It was originally a method used by thieves to entrap their pedestrians and subsequently rob them. One thief would be assigned 'tripper up' duty, and would use different instruments to knock the person to the ground. Luckily, these days the saying is much more friendlier, though being on the end of a joke might not always be fun.

2. "Bark up the wrong tree"

Definition: To make the wrong choice or pursue the wrong course.

Origin: When hunting raccoons for fur was a popular sport, hunting dogs were used to sniff them out of trees. Being a nocturnal animal, the hunting party had to work at night, and the dogs would sometimes end up choosing the wrong tree, or as the idiom goes, 'bark up the wrong tree". The term was first printed in a book by Davy Crockett in 1833.

3. "Bite the bullet"

Definition: If a person bites the bullet, it means that they take whatever punishment they must in order to end something.

Origin: This came about during war times, probably the Civil War. With very little anesthetic available, patients were operated upon with nothing to numb the pain or to render them unconscious. A large number of these operations were amputations. The surgeon would literally saw off a limb. The patient was given a bullet to put in their mouth to bite down on when they felt pain. It was used to give the patient something to focus upon and probably also to cut down on screaming so as not to frighten other patients or disrupt the surgeon. Bullets were used simply because they were readily available and didn't break the teeth. So when a patient agreed to bite the bullet, they believed that the surgery was necessary despite the pain and just wanted to get it finished.

4. "It's raining cats and dogs"

Definition: People say it's raining cats and dogs when there is a heavy rainstorm.

Origin: This originates from the medieval times. People threw their trash out in the gutters. When their pets died, they were dumped in the same way. When a heavy rain occurred that flooded the gutters, the cats and dogs were washed out in the streets. So, a heavy rain came to be linked with cats and dogs.

5. "Pass the buck"

Definition: This means to pass the responsibility onto another person.

Origin: This idiom's origins are from gambling circles. During card games, the dealer had a marker called a buck. It is thought that it was called a buck because it was usually a buck-handled knife. When the round of cards was over, the 'buck' was passed on to the next player, and so the responsibility of dealing was also passed on. Later, perhaps for safety reasons, the knife was replaced with a silver dollar. It is thought that this is how 'buck' became slang for a dollar.

6. "Sleep tight"

Definition: Sleep tight means to have a good night's sleep.

Origin: Bed frames used to be made from ropes. The ropes would get loose and made sleeping very uncomfortable. The ropes would have to be tightened each night in order to sleep well. So came about the saying to 'sleep tight.'

7. "Who let the cat out of the bag?"

Definition: This saying means that someone exposed a secret.

Origin: Its origins are from street markets from medieval times. Chickens or pigs were sold tied up in a bag. But often, dishonest sellers would substitute cats for the chickens and pigs. If a customer opened the bag before the transaction was settled, they would realize that they had been cheated and the secret would be known.

Pay attention to your conversations. You will be surprised how often you and others utter nonsensical idioms that actually have interesting history behind them!

CHAPTER XXIX

Funny English

1. By an Educationist

There is this educationist in Chennai who is very popular for this excellent :-) English skills. When I read them from time to time, I honestly thought that they were all exaggerated because someone simply cannot talk like this! But, some of my friends swore that they were all true and these were collated by his own students. Anyway, whether this is true or all cooked up, this gentleman has given me some pure entertainment on the net!.

Here are samples of his English during his interactions with students in his colleges. You will enjoy these more if you know a bit of the Tamil language as well.

At the playground

All of you stand in a straight circle

There is no wind in the balloon.

The girl with the mirror please come here...(meaning, girl with spectacles, please come here).

To a boy, angrily

I talk, he talk, why you middle middle talk?

While punishing students

You, rotate the ground four times...

You, go and understand the tree...

You three of you stand together separately.

Why are you late - say YES or NO .....(?)

At his best

He once went to a movie with his wife, and happened to see one of his students at the theatre though the boy did not notice them.

The next day at college, he said (to that boy) - "Yesterday I saw you with my wife at the cinema theatre" ...(?)

At his best inside the Classroom

Open the doors of the window. Let the atmosphere come in.

Open the doors of the window. Let the air force come in.

Cut an apple into two halves - I will take the bigger half.

Shh.. quiet boys.. the principal **just passed away** in the corridor

You, meet me behind the class (meaning **after** the class)

This one is cool - Both of you three get out of the class!

Close the doors of the windows please. I have winter in my nose today....

Take Copper wire of any metal, especially Silver...

Take 5 cm wire of any length...

At College

This college strict you the worry no....you get good marks, I the happy, tomorrow you get good job, I am happy, tomorrow you marry I the enjoy" (?)

No ragging this college. Anybody rag we arrest the police.

About his family :

I have two daughters. Both of them are girls...(?)

More...

Once he had come late to a college function, and by the time he arrived, the function had begun,. So he went to the dais, and said, sorry I am late, because on the way my car hit 2 muttons (meaning goats!!).

- When the students were on a strike inside the college, someone hit him with a pen... he then said... "I court order strictly follow. You kill I?"
- All standing under the tree whos whos class whos whos go
- Boy Boy talk... Girl Girl talk... No boy girl talk... If talk punish Boy – very famous one!
- Boy boy talk no problem... Girl girl talk no problem... Boy girl talk everything problem!
- His speech about Kargil widows: "All brothers standing border... shooting, dying... child asking mummy... "Mummy, where is daddy"... Daddy coming body! Saying this he wiped his tears...
- Once he saw a student wearing a cap and said "In campus, cap no use"
- These were the words he spoke on a Teacher's day... on every Teacher's day – "A doctor cannot make a doctor; A lawyer cannot make a layer; Engineer cannot make engineer; A teacher can maker doctor, lawyer, engineer, teacher"

2. Resume Writing

People write the strangest things on their resumes, sometimes downright hysterical. Why should only recruiting managers get to laugh at these? Enjoy!

"I have a graduate degree in unclear physics."

"My hobbies include raising long-eared rabbis as pets."

"Career break in 1999 to renovate my horse"

"1990 – 1997: Stewardess – Royal Air Force"

Hobbies: "enjoy cooking Chinese and Italians"

"Service for old man to check they are still alive or not."

Cleaning skills: "bleaching, pot washing, window cleaning, mopping, e.t.c"

"Job involved...counselling clientele on accidental insurance policies available"

"2001 summer voluntary work for taking care of the elderly and vegetable people"

"I'm interested to here more about that. I'm working today in a furniture factory as a drawer"

"I am about to enroll on a Business and Finance Degree with the Open University. I feel that this qualification will prove detrimental to me for future success."

"Time is very valuable and it should be always used to achieve optimum results and I believe it should not be played around with"

"My last job was as a plumbing and hating specialists."

"I worked for 6 years as an uninformed security guard."

"I believe that weakness is the first level of strength, given the right attitude and driving force. My school advised me to fix my punctuality.

"This has reference to your advertisement calling for a ' Typist and an Accountant – Male or Female'... As I am both (!!) for the past several years and I can handle both with good experience, I am applying for the post.

3. Cover Letters

The following quotations were taken from cover letters. It is unfortunate that such mistakes slip through to the final draft, and make exactly the wrong impression on exactly the wrong people.

- "Thank you for your consideration. Hope to hear from you shorty!"
- "Enclosed is a ruff draft of my resume."

- "I saw your ad on the information highway, and I came to a screeching halt."
- "Please disregard the attached resume -- it is terribly out of date."
- "It's best for employers that I not work with people."
- "Insufficient writing skills, thought processes have slowed down some. If I am not one of the best, I will look for another opportunity."
- "If this resume doesn't blow your hat off, then please return it in the enclosed envelope."
- "My fortune cookie said, 'Your next interview will result in a job' -- and I like your company in particular."
- "You hold in your hands the resume of a truly outstanding candidate!"
- "I am sicking and entry-level position."
- "Here are my qualifications for you to overlook."
- "I am a quick leaner, dependable, and motivated."
- "I am relatively intelligent, obedient, and as loyal as a puppy."
- "Note: Keep this resume on top of the stack. Use all the others to heat your house."
- "I don't usually blow my own horn, but in this case, I will go right ahead and do so."
- "I need just enough money to have pizza every night."
- "My compensation should be at least equal to my age."
- "I'm submitting my resume to spite my lack of C++ and HTML experience."
- "My primary goal is to be recognized."
- "Below are the top 10 reasons to hire me."
- "I am superior to anyone else you could hire."
- "I vow to fulfill the goals of the company as long as I live."
- "Although I am seeking an accounting job, the fact that I have no actual experience in accounting may seem discouraging. However..."
- "I realize that my total lack of appropriate experience may concern those considering me for employment."
- "I worked here full-time there."
- "I'll starve without a job but don't feel you have to give me one."
- "You are privileged to receive my resume

4. Matrimonial Ads

I bet you can't stop laughing after reading this. These are actual ads on a matrimony site. (I'm skipping the name...) Grammar and spelling errors

have no place in a profile description as everything is straight from the heart
.

****

Hello To Viewers My Name is Sowmya , I am single i dont have male,I f any one whant to marrie to me u can visite to my home. I am not a good education but i working all field in bangalore .. if u like me u welcome to my heart... when ever u whant to meet pls visit my resident or send u letter..
Thanks
yours Regards Sowmya
(Truly yours)

****

i want very simple boy. from brahmin educated family from Orissa state she is also know about RAMAYAN, GEETA BHAGABATA, and other homework
What Homework???

****

I am a happy-go-lucky kind of person. Enjoys every moments of life. I love to make friendship. Becauese friendship is a first step of love. I am looking for my dreamboy who will love me more than i. Because i love myself a lot. If u think that is u then why to late come on........hold my hand forever !!!
(The dilwale dulhaniya effect)

****

i am simple girl. I have lot of problem in my life because of my luck. now i am looking one boy he care me and love me lot lot lot
(Lot lot...??)

****

i want a boy with no drinks if he wants he can wear jeans in house but while steping out of house he should give recpect to our cast
(by not wearing his jeans? What the hell...)

****

HYE I AM A GOOD LOKING GIRL,WHO HAS THE CAPABILITY TO MAKE ANY BODY TO
LOUGH.I BELIEVE IN GOD AND ACCORDING TO ME FRIENDS ARE THE REAL
MESSENGER OF GOD. THE 3 THINGS I AM LOOKING FROM A BOY THEY ARE
1. THEY MUST BELIEVE IN GOD.

2. THEY HAVE TO LIKE MY PROFFESION
3. THEY SHOULD NOT GET BORED WITH ME WHEN I WILL TRY
TO MAKE THEM LOUGH.
(all of us are loughing {laughing})

****

whatever he may be but he should feel that he is going to be someone groom and he must think of the future life if he is toolike this he would be called the man of the lamp
(She want's a lamp...?)

****

i love my patner i marriage the patner ok i search my patner and I love the patner ok thik hai the patner has a graduate ok
(The person seems to be suffering from 'Ok-syndrome')

****

iam pranati my family histoy my two brother two sister and father & Mother. sister completely married
(somebody please explain how to get married completely'?)

****

my name is farhanbegum and i am unmarried. pleaes you marrige me pleaes pleaes pleaes pleaes pleaes pleaes pleaes
(Height of desperation!)

****

iam kanandevi. i do own businas.one sistar. he was marred.
(No comments)

****

I am Sharmila my colour is black, but my heart is white. i like social service.
(Zebra..???)

****

Wants a woman who knows me better and can adjust with me forever. she may never create any difficulties in my life or her life by which the entire life can run smoothly. thank you
(The principle of running life smoothly was never so easy!)

****

she should be good looking and should have a service. she Should have one brother and one sister. she should be educated.
(ain't it unique !! 1 brother 1 sister criteria !)

****

iam very simpel and hanest. i have three sister one brother and parent. iam doing postal sarvice and tailor master my original resdence at kalahandi diste naw iam staing at rayagada dist.

(actually what is this guy doing? Postal service or tailor.??)

****

Iwant one girl who love me or my mother. she love me heartly or she havea frank she's skin colour 'normal'not a black or not a whitey. IThink the main think is heart if your heart is beautiful then you are beautiful. but iam not a handsome guy or not a good looking. but my Mom say that

Iam a good guy. My father already expired . THE CHOICE IS YOUR. bye bye.

(uttama purushan)

****

i'm looking out for who lives in bombay , girl simple who trust me lot should be roman catholic, LOVE ME ONLY.
(Now that criterion is a must, isn't it?)

****

to be married on jan-2006. working woman perferable
(this guy has fixed the marriage date too!)

****

i would like a beautyfull girl. and i do not want her any treasure. because girl is the maharani.

(Now she is going to be a lucky girl! Any takers?)

****

5. Notices

Here are some genuine examples of imperfect, but amusing English found around the world.

At a Budapest zoo
PLEASE DO NOT FEED THE ANIMALS. IF YOU HAVE ANY SUITABLE FOOD, GIVE IT TO THE GUARD ON DUTY.

Cocktail lounge, Norway
LADIES ARE REQUESTED NOT TO HAVE CHILDREN IN THE BAR.

Hotel, Acapulco
THE MANAGER HAS PERSONALLY PASSED ALL THE WATER SERVED HERE.

Car rental brochure, Tokyo

WHEN PASSENGER OF FOOT HEAVE IN SIGHT, TOOTLE THE HORN. TRUMPET HIM MELODIOUSLY AT FIRST, BUT IF HE STILL OBSTACLES YOUR PASSAGE THEN TOOTLE HIM WITH VIGOUR.

In a Nairobi restaurant

CUSTOMERS WHO FIND OUR WAITRESSES RUDE OUGHT TO SEE THE MANAGER.

On the grounds of a private school

NO TRESPASSING WITHOUT PERMISSION.

In a City restaurant

OPEN SEVEN DAYS A WEEK, AND WEEKENDS TOO.

A sign seen on an automatic restroom hand dryer

DO NOT ACTIVATE WITH WET HANDS.

In a Indian maternity ward

NO CHILDREN ALLOWED.

In a cemetery

PERSONS ARE PROHIBITED FROM PICKING FLOWERS FROM ANY BUT THEIR OWN GRAVES.

On the menu of a Swiss restaurant

OUR WINES LEAVE YOU NOTHING TO HOPE FOR.

Hotel brochure, Italy

THIS HOTEL IS RENOWNED FOR ITS PEACE AND SOLITUDE. IN FACT, CROWDS FROM ALL OVER THE WORLD FLOCK HERE TO ENJOY ITS SOLITUDE.

Hotel lobby, Romania

THE LIFT IS BEING FIXED FOR THE NEXT DAY. DURING THAT TIME WE REGRET THAT YOU WILL BE UNBEARABLE.

In the lobby of a Moscow hotel across from a Russian Orthodox monastery

YOU ARE WELCOME TO VISIT THE CEMETERY WHERE FAMOUS RUSSIAN AND SOVIET COMPOSERS, ARTISTS, AND WRITERS ARE BURIED DAILY EXCEPT THURSDAY.

Taken from a menu, Poland

SALAD A FIRM'S OWN MAKE; LIMPID RED BEET SOUP WITH CHEESY DUMPLINGS IN THE FORM OF A FINGER; ROASTED DUCK LET LOOSE; BEEF RASHERS BEATEN IN THE COUNTRY PEOPLE'S FASHION.

Supermarket, Hong Kong

FOR YOUR CONVENIENCE, WE RECOMMEND COURTEOUS, EFFICIENT SELF-SERVICE.

In an East African newspaper

A NEW SWIMMING POOL IS RAPIDLY TAKING SHAPE SINCE THE CONTRACTORS HAVE THROWN IN THE BULK OF THEIR WORKERS.

Hotel, Vienna

IN CASE OF FIRE, DO YOUR UTMOST TO ALARM THE HOTEL PORTER.

An advertisement by a Hong Kong dentist

TEETH EXTRACTED BY THE LATEST METHODISTS.

Tourist agency, former Czechoslovakia

TAKE ONE OF OUR HORSE-DRIVEN CITY TOURS. WE GUARANTEE NO MISCARRIAGES.

The box of a clockwork toy made in Hong Kong

GUARANTEED TO WORK THROUGHOUT ITS USEFUL LIFE.

In a Swiss mountain inn

Special today - No Ice-Cream

Airline ticket office, Copenhagen

We take your bags and send them in all directions

In a Tokyo Hotel

Is forbidden to steal hotel towels please. If you are not a person to do such thing is please not to read notis.

In a Leipzig elevator

Do not enter the lift backwards, and only when lit up.

In a Belgrade hotel elevator

To move the cabin, push button for wishing floor. If the cabin should enter more persons, each one should press a number of wishing floor. Driving is then going alphabetically by national order.

In a Paris hotel elevator

Please leave your values at the front desk.

In a hotel in Athens

Visitors are expected to complain at the office between the hours of 9 and 11 A.M. daily.

In a Rhodes tailor shop

Order your summers suit. Because in big rush we will execute customers in strict rotation.

6. *Letter to God*

Little Leroy came into the kitchen where his mother was making dinner. His birthday was coming up and he thought this was a good time to tell his mother what he wanted.

"Mom, I want a bike for my birthday." Little Leroy was a bit of a troublemaker. He had gotten into trouble at school and at home. Leroy's mother asked him if he thought he deserved to get a bike for his birthday. Little Leroy, of course, thought he did.

Leroy's mother, being a Christian woman, wanted him to reflect on his behavior over the last year and write a letter to God and tell him why he deserved a bike for his birthday.

LETTER 1:
Dear God,
I have been a very good boy this year and I would like a bike for my birthday.
I want a red one.
Your friend, Leroy
Leroy knew this wasn't true. He had not been a very good boy this year, so he tore up the letter and started over.

LETTER 2:
Dear God,
This is your friend Leroy. I have been a pretty good boy this year, and I would like a red bike for my birthday.
Thank you,
Leroy
Leroy knew this wasn't true either. He tore up the letter and started again.

LETTER 3:
Dear God,
I have been an OK boy this year and I would really like a red bike for my birthday.
Leroy
Leroy knew he could not send this letter to God either .
Leroy was very upset.He went downstairs and told his mother he wanted

to go church. Leroy's mother thought her plan had worked because Leroy looked very sad. "Just be home in time for dinner," his mother said.
Leroy walked down the street to the church and up to the altar. He looked around to see if anyone was there. He picked up a statue of the Virgin Mary. He slipped it under his shirt and ran out of the church, down the street, into his house, and up to his room. He shut the door to his room and sat down with a piece of paper and a pen.Leroy began to write his letter to God.

LETTER 4:
I'VE GOT YOUR MOM. IF YOU WANT TO SEE HER AGAIN, SEND THE BIKE.
Signed
YOU KNOW WHO

7. Leave letters

Some amusing leave letters....

An employee in a software company applied for leave as follows:

"Since I have to go to my village to sell my land along with my wife, please sanction me one-week leave."

From an employee who was performing the "mundan" ceremony of his 10 year old son.

"as I want to shave my son's head, please leave me for two days.."

Another one from an employee who was performing his daughter's wedding:

"as I am marrying my daughter, please grant a week's leave.."

From H.A.L. Administration Dept:

"As my mother-in-law has expired and I am only one responsible for it, please grant me 10 days leave."

Another employee applied for half day leave as follows:

"Since I've to go to the cremation ground at 10 o-clock and I may not return, please grant me half day casual leave"

An incident of a leave letter

"I am suffering from fever, please declare one-day holiday."

A leave letter to the headmaster

"As I am studying in this school I am suffering from headache. I request you to leave me today"

Another leave letter written to the headmaster:

"As my headache is paining, please grant me leave for the day."

Another leave letter application
"My wife is suffering from sickness and as I am her only husband at home I may be granted leave".

8. Funny Newspaper Ads

There are often more laughs on the advertising and classified pages than you can find in the cartoons and comic strips. Here are some samples....

FREE YORKSHIRE TERRIER.
  8 years old. Hateful little dog. Bites.

FREE PUPPIES:
1/2 Cocker Spaniel, 1/2 sneaky neighbor's dog.

FREE PUPPIES...
Mother, AKC German Shepherd.
Father, Super Dog...able to leap tall fences in a single bound.

FOUND DIRTY WHITE DOG.
Looks like a rat ... Been out a while.
Better be a reward.

WEDDING DRESS FOR SALE.
WORN ONCE BY MISTAKE.
Call Stephanie.

AND THE BEST ONE:

FOR SALE BY OWNER:
Complete set of Encyclopedia Britannica, 45 volumes.
Excellent condition. $1,000 or best offer. No longer needed, got
married last month. Wife knows everything.
  More amusing newspaper ads....

• For sale: an antique desk suitable for lady with thick legs and large
  drawers.

- Now is your chance to have your ears pierced and get an extra pair to take home, too.
- We do not tear your clothing with machinery. We do it carefully by hand.
- Used Cars: Why go elsewhere to be cheated? Come here first!
- 3-year-old teacher needed for pre-school. Experience preferred.
- Mother's helper--peasant working conditions.
- We will oil your sewing machine and adjust tension in your home for $1.00.

9. Indianism's in English Language

This is not an attempt to fix all the grammatical expressions in common Indian English. These samples are just to illustrate our typical style of English conversations. Let us try to correct them atleast now.

'**Years back**' is one among them. 'Years back' expression is used to mean that 'a thing that happened years ago'. If it happened in the past, it happened years ago, not "years back." Given how common this phrase is, may be the first person who switched "ago" for "back" probably did it years back. Got it?

'**Passing Out**' is another hilarious Indian English phrase used by Indians. People use it in the sense that a person has completed the studies from an educational institution. We can say one graduated from the institute. When you complete your studies at an educational institution, you graduate from that institution. To "pass out' refers to losing consciousness, like after you get too drunk!

'**Discuss about**', another great mistake committed by us. You don't "discuss about" something; you just discuss things. The word "discuss" means to "talk about". There is no reason to insert the word "about" after "discuss."

'**Kindly revert**' is also a mistake usually committed to mean reply or respond. But the actual meaning of revert means that "to return to the former condition or practice". Thinking of the actual meaning we can find that what a blunder is to say things like, "Please revert at the latest."

'**Doing the needful**' is a style that has become outdated decades ago, the time the British left. "Do the needful" is an archaic expression that is used humorously which denotes that to 'do things which is necessary'.

'**Do one thing**' is also an expression which doesn't make any sense. When someone approaches you with a query, and your reply begins with the phrase "do one thing," you're doing it wrong. This Indianism is not at all a proper English word and hence it is better to avoid while speaking. There are better ways to begin a reply. And worst of all, any person who starts a sentence with "do one thing" invariably ends up giving you at least five things to do.

Sample - " My computer keeps getting hung."

"Do one thing. Clear your history. Delete your cookies. Run a virus check. Restart your computer... ."

'**Out of station**', another funny expression used by Indians to say that "I'm away from home." Another blast from the past, this one, and also, extremely outdated. What's wrong with "out of town" or "not in Mumbai" or "I'm not here"?

'**Order for**' is an Indian phrasal usage extremely wrong in proper English. We usually say, "Let's order for a tea." The best thing one can do is that when one needs something, "order" it, try not to "order for" it.

'**Prepone**' is used by Indians in the sense that to advance something. It might be used in an assumption that the opposite of postpone is prepone. We say, "Let's prepone the discussion from 1PM to 11PM." We can actually say "Could we bring the meeting forward."

The big sleep

"I'm going to bed now, sleep is coming." This is really taking things a bit too far...! Don't you think?

Taking things

"I will call you back later as I am taking my lunch right now."

Taking it where? To the pool for a swim?

Just like "take rest."

Really. "Take rest." Instead of just "rest." Why?

It seems that we just love to take things. Where do we put them?

Putting this and that

"Put on the switch", "Put this yellow dress."

We just love using the word "put." It's a great so-called filler verb to shorten sentences.

"Switch on/turn on the light" or "wear/put on this yellow dress" are all correct.

No idea how "put" came into the picture.

10. Scrabbles

Check out these deadly Scrabbles. Someone out there is really good at them, or has too much time on their hands.

DILIP VENGSARKAR
When you rearrange the letters:
SPARKLING DRIVE

PRINCESS DIANA
When you rearrange the letters:
END IS A CAR SPIN

MONICA LEWINSKY
When you rearrange the letters:
NICE SILKY WOMAN

DORMITORY:
When you rearrange the letters:
DIRTY ROOM

ASTRONOMER:
When you rearrange the letters:
MOON STARER

DESPERATION:
When you rearrange the letters:
A ROPE ENDS IT

THE EYES:
When you rearrange the letters:
THEY SEE

GEORGE BUSH:
When you rearrange the letters:
HE BUGS GORE

THE MORSE CODE :

When you rearrange the letters:
HERE COME DOTS

SLOT MACHINES:
When you rearrange the letters:
CASH LOST IN ME
    ANIMOSITY:
When you rearrange the letters:
IS NO AMITY
    ELECTION RESULTS:
When you rearrange the letters:
LIES - LET'S RECOUNT
    SNOOZE ALARMS:
When you rearrange the letters:
ALAS! NO MORE Z 'S
    A DECIMAL POINT:
When you rearrange the letters:
IM A DOT IN PLACE
    THE EARTHQUAKES:
When you rearrange the letters:
THAT QUEER SHAKE
    ELEVEN PLUS TWO:
When you rearrange the letters:
TWELVE PLUS ONE
    MOTHER-IN-LAW:
When you rearrange the letters:
WOMAN HITLER
    EVANGELIST
    When you rearrange the letters:
    EVIL'S AGENT
    ELEVEN PLUS TWO:
    When you rearrange the letters:
    TWELVE PLUS ONE
    PRESIDENT CLINTON OF THE USA:
    When you rearrange the letters (with no letters left over and using each letter only once):
TO COPULATE HE FINDS INTERNS

11. Palindromes

Palindromes are words, phrases or number sequences that read the same way in both directions, left-to-right, and right-to-left. **Palindrome** derives from the Greek for 'running back again'. Both the Greeks and Romans are known to have enjoyed palindromes. The Greeks also published palindromic poetry.

Single Word Palindromes

Some single word palindromes are: level, racecar, rotator, pip, radar, nun, mom, toot, deed, civic, eye, pop, malayalam, madam

Phrase Palindromes

A phrase that is palandomic is "never odd or even." Read this phrase right-to-left, rearranging the spaces. Two other examples are "a Toyota," and "Was it a rat I saw?"

Number Palindromes

Some example of palindromic numbers are: 55, 484, 3003, 29592

Isn't this interesting? Do your research for more Palindromes...

12. Telegrams

TELEGRAM #1

A blonde a brunette are running a ranch together in Louisiana. They decide they need a bull to mate with their cows to increase their herd. The brunette takes their life savings of $600 and goes to Texas to buy a bull.

She eventually meets with an old cowboy that will sell her a bull. "It's the only one I got for $599, take it or leave it." She buys the bull and goes to the local telegram office and says, "I'd like to send a telegram to my friend in Louisiana that says: "Have found the stud bull for our ranch. Bring the trailer."

The man behind the counter tells her, "Telegrams to anywhere in the U.S. are 75 cents per word."

She thinks about it for a moment and decides. "I'd like to send one word, please."

"And what word would that be?" inquires the man.

"Comfortable," replies the brunette.

The man asks, "I'm sorry miss, but how is your friend gonna understand this telegram?"

The brunette replies, "My friend is blonde and reads REAL slow. When she gets this, she will see COM-FOR-DA-BULL."

TELEGRAM #2

A husband, while he is on a business trip to a hill station sends a telegram to his wife: "I wish you were here."

The message received by wife:

"I wish you were her."

TELEGRAM #3

A wife with near maturing pregnancy goes to railway station to return to her husband. At the reservation counter, while her turn came, it was the last ticket. Taking pity on a very old lady next to her in the queue,she offered her berth to the old lady and sent a telegram to her husband which reached as:

"Shall be coming tomorrow, heavy rush in the train, gave birth to an old lady."

TELEGRAM #4

A man from Agra went to Ajmer . His wife was in her parent's house in Delhi .

When the man went to Ajmer , he asked his servant to send a telegram to his wife indicating about his trip to Ajmer .He sent a telegram. When the wife received the telegram, she fainted.

It was written:

'Sethji aaj mar gaye! (Sethji Ajmer gaye).

13. Office Designations

Here are some funny definitions of designations at office.

Project Manager - A person who thinks nine women can deliver a baby in one month.

Developer - A person who thinks it will take 18 months to deliver a baby.

Onsite Coordinator - Who thinks single woman can deliver nine babies in one month.

Client - The one who doesn't know why he wants a baby.

Marketing Manager - Is a person who thinks he can deliver a baby even if no man and woman are available.

Resource Optimization Team - Think they don't need a man or woman; they'll produce a child with zero resources.

Documentation Team - They don't care whether the child is delivered, they'll just document 9 months.

Quality Auditor - Who is never happy with the process to produce a baby.

Tester - A person who always tells his wife that this is not the right baby and lastly..............

HR Manager - A person who thinks that a donkey can deliver a human baby – if given 9 months!!

14. Longest Word

Longest Word in the English Language without Repeating Letters

The two 15 letter words **uncopyrightable & dermatoglyphics** are the words in the English language which do not have any letter repeated.

Uncopyrightable : This word in simple terms means ineligible for copyright.

Dermatoglyphics : This word refers to the study of fingerprints and toe prints.

Longest Word with All Vowels in Order

The 23 letter word ' **Pancreaticoduodenostomy**' happens to be the longest word in the English language which has all vowels in order of 'a, e, i, o, u'. This word Pancreaticoduodenostomy means a formation of an opening connecting the pancreas to the duodenum artificially by surgery.

Longest Word in which all letters Appear Twice

The 16 letter word ' **Esophagographers**' is the longest word in the English language that has all letters appearing twice! Quite an intriguing fact! An esophagographer is a person conducting the radiographic visualization of the food pipe of esophagus.

Longest Word with letters in Alphabetical Order

We have an amazing 8 letter word in the English language that consists of all its letters in alphabetical order. This word is ' **aegilops**', which in the medical dictionary stands for the fistula formed in the inner corner of the eye. In botanical terms it stands for great wild-oat grass.

Longest Word in the English Language

According to the Oxford Dictionary, the title of the longest word in the English language goes to the 45 letter word, **'Pneumonoultramicroscopicsilicovolcanoconiosis'.**

Coined in 1935 by Everett M. Smith, the then president of the National Puzzlers' League, at its annual meeting, the word **Pneumonoultramicroscopicsilicovolcanoconiosis** is the name of a respiratory lung disease conduced by increased exposure to silica dust. Inhalation of microscopic silicone dust particles expelled from volcanic eruptions leads to this respiratory disease. Pronunciation of this word is difficult because of its length and for those with the fear of long words or Hippopotomonstrosesquippedaliophobia, this word seems to be all the more intimidating.

However, if we break it up it will become easier. Consider the pronunciation break up:

NYOO-muh-noh-ul-truh-my-kruh- skop-ik-SIL-i-koh-vol-kay-noh-koh-nee-OH-siss

15. Truth about Letters

Did you appreciate the truth about letters?

Letters 'a', 'b', 'c' and 'd' do not appear if you spell any of the numbers between 1 and 99

[Funnily enough, letter 'd' comes for the first time in Hundred]

In addition, letters 'a', 'b' and 'c' do not appear anywhere in the spellings of 1 to 999

[Strange, but true, letter 'a' comes for the first time in Thousand]

Neither letter 'b' nor 'c' appear anywhere in the spellings of 1 to 999,999,999

[Letter 'b' comes for the first time in Billion]

Letter 'c' does not appear anywhere in the spellings of entire English counting

CHAPTER XXX

200 Secrets of Success

by Robin S. Sharma

1. Sleep less. This is one of the best investments you can make to make your life more productive and rewarding. Most people do not need more than 6 hours to maintain an excellent state of health. Try getting up one hour earlier for 21 days and it will develop into a powerful habit. Remember, it is the quality not the quantity of sleep that is important. And just imagine having an extra 30 hours a month to spend on the things that are important to you.

2. Set aside one hour every morning for personal development matters. Meditate, visualize your day, read inspirational texts to set the tone of your day, listen to motivational tapes or read great literature. Take this quiet period to vitalize and energize your spirit for the productive day ahead. Watch the sun rise once a week or be with nature. Starting the day off well is a powerful strategy for self-renewal and personal effectiveness.

3. Do not allow those things that matter the most in your life be at the mercy of activities that matter the least. Every day, take the time to ask yourself the question "is this the best use of my time and energy?" Time management is life management so guard your time with great care.

4. Use the rubber band method to condition your mind to focus solely on the most positive elements in your life. Place a rubber band around your wrist. Each time a negative, energy sapping thought enters your mind, snap the rubber band. Through the power of conditioning, your mind will associate pain with negative thinking and you will soon possess a strongly positive mindset.

5. Always answer the phone with enthusiasm in your voice and show your appreciation for the caller. Good phone manners are essential. To convey authority on the line, stand up. This will instill further confidence in your

voice.

6. Throughout the day we all get inspiration and excellent ideas. Keep a set of cards (the size of business cards; available at most stationary stores) in your wallet along with a pencil to jot down these insights. When you get home, put the ideas in a central place such as a coil notepad and review them from time to time. As noted by Oliver Wendell Holmes: "Man's mind, once stretched by a new idea, never regains its original dimensions."

7. Set aside every Sunday evening for yourself and be strongly disciplined with this habit. Use this period to plan your week, visualize your encounters and what you want to achieve, to read new materials and inspirational books, to listen to soft soothing music and to simply relax. This habit will serve as your anchor to keep you focused, motivated and effective throughout the coming week.

8. Always remember the key principle that the quality of your life is the quality of your communication. This means the way you communicate with others and, more importantly, the way you communicate with yourself. What you focus on is what you get. If you look for the positive this is what you get. This is a fundamental law of Nature.

9. Stay on purpose, not on outcome. In other words, do the task because it is what you love to do or because it will help someone or is a valuable exercise. Don't do it for the money or the recognition. Those will come naturally. This is the way of the world.

10. Laugh for five minutes in the mirror each morning. Steve Martin does. Laughter activates many beneficial chemicals within the body that place us into a very joyous state. Laughter also returns the body to a state of balance. Laughter therapy has been regularly used to heal persons with varied ailments and is a wonderful tonic for life's ills. While the average 4 year old laughs 500 times a day, the average adult is lucky to laugh 15 times a day. Revitalize the habit of laughter, it will put far more living into your life.

11. Light a candle beside you when you are reading in the evening. It is most relaxing and creates a wonderful, soothing atmosphere. Make your home an

oasis from the frenzied world outside. Fill it with great music, great books and great friends.

12. To enhance your concentration and powers of focus, count your steps when you walk. This is a particularly strong technique. Take six steps while taking a long inhale, hold your breath for another six steps, and then exhale for six steps. If six steps is too long for the breaths, do whatever you feel comfortable with. You will feel very alert, refreshed, internally quiet and centered after this exercise. So many people allow their minds to be filled with mental chatter. All peak performers appreciate the power of a quiet, clear mind which will concentrate steadily on all important tasks.

13. Learn to meditate effectively. The mind is naturally a very noisy machine which wants to move from one subject to another like an unchained monkey. One must learn to restrain and discipline it if one is to achieve anything of substance and to be peaceful. Meditation for twenty minutes in the morning and twenty minutes in the evening will certainly provide you with exceptional results if regularly practiced for six months. Learned sages of the East have been advancing the many benefits of meditation for over 5000 years.

14. Learn to be still. The average person doesn't spend even 30 minutes a month in total silence and tranquility. Develop the skill of sitting quietly, enjoying the powerful silence for at least ten minutes a day. Simply think about what is important to you in your life. Reflect on your mission. Silence indeed is golden. As the Zen master once said, it is the space between the bars that holds the cage.

15. Enhance your will-power; it is likely one of the best training programs you can invest in. Here are some ideas to strengthen your will and become a stronger person:

a. Do not let your mind float like a piece of paper in the wind. Work hard to keep it focused at all times. When doing a task, think of nothing else. When walking to work, count the steps that it takes to get all the way to the office. This is not easy but your mind will soon understand that you hold its reins and not vice versa. Your mind must eventually become as still as a candle flame in a corner where there is no draft.

b. Your will is like a muscle. You must first exercise it and then push before it gets stronger. This necessarily involves short term pain but be assured that the improvements will come and will touch your character in a most positive way. When you are hungry, wait another hour before your meal. When you are labouring over a difficult task and your mind is prompting you to pick up the latest magazine for a break or to get up and go talk to a friend, curb the impulse. Soon you will be able to sit for hours in a precisely concentrated state. Sir Issac Newton, one of the greatest classical physicists the world has produced, once said: "if I have done the public any service, it is due to patient thought." Newton had a remarkable ability to sit quietly and think without interruption for very long periods of time. If he can develop this so can you.

c. You can also build your will-power by restraint in your conduct with others. Speak less (use the 60/40 Rule = listen 60% of the time and speak a mere 40%, if that). This will not only make you more popular but you will learn much wisdom as everyone we meet, every day has something to teach us. Also restrain the urge to gossip or to condemn someone who you feel has made a mistake. Stop complaining and develop a cheerful, vital and strong personality. You will greatly influence others.

d. When a negative thought comes to your mind, immediately replace it with one that is positive. Positive always dominates over the negative and your mind has to be conditioned to think only the best thoughts. Negative thinking is a conditioned process whereby the negative patterns are established over and over. Rid yourself of any limitations and become a powerful positive thinker.

16. Make an effort to be humorous throughout the day. Not only is it beneficial from a physical viewpoint but it diffuses tension in difficult circumstances and creates an excellent atmosphere wherever you are. It was recently reported that members of the Tauripan tribe of South America have a ritual where they awake in the middle of the night to tell each other jokes. Even tribesmen in the deepest sleep wake to enjoy the laugh and then return to their state of slumber in seconds.

17. Become a highly disciplined time manager. There are roughly 168 hours in a week. This surely allows plenty of time for achievement of the many goals we desire to accomplish. Be ruthless with your time. Set aside a few minutes each morning to plan your day. Plan around your priorities and focus on not only those tasks which are immediate but not important (i.e., many telephone calls) but especially on those which are important but not urgent, for these allow for the greatest personal and professional development. Important but not immediate activities are those which produce long-term, sustainable benefits and include exercise, strategic planning, the development of relationships and professional education. Never let the things which matter most be placed in the backseat as compared to those that matter least.

18. Associate only with positive, focused people who you can learn from and who will not drain your valuable energy with complaining and uninspiring attitudes. By developing relationships with those committed to constant improvement and the pursuit of the best that life has to offer, you will have plenty of company on your path to the top of whatever mountain you seek to climb.

19. Stephen Hawking, one of the great modern physicists of the world, is reported to have said that we are on a minor planet of a very average star located within the outer limits of one of a hundred thousand million galaxies. Are your problems really significant in light of this? You walk this Earth for but a short time. Why not become devoted to having only a wonderful experience. Why not dedicate yourself to leaving a powerful legacy to the world? Sit down now and write out a list of all that you have in your life. Start first with your health or your family - the things we often take for granted. Put down the country we live in and the food we eat. Do not stop until you have written down fifty items. Once every few days, go through this list - you will be uplifted and recognize the richness of your existence.

20. You must have a mission statement in life. This is simply a set of guiding principles which clearly state where you are going and where you want to be at the end of your life. A mission statement embodies your values. It is your personal lighthouse keeping you steadily on the course of your

dreams. Over a period of one month, set a few hours aside to write down five or ten principles which will govern your life and which will keep you focused at all times. Examples might be to consistently serve others, to be a considerate citizen, to become highly wealthy or to serve as a powerful leader. Whatever the mission statement of your life, refine it and review it regularly. Then when something adverse happens or someone tries to pull you off course, you quickly and precisely return to your chosen path with the full knowledge that you are moving in the direction that you have selected.

21. No one can insult or hurt you without your permission. One of the golden keys to happiness and great success is the way you interpret events which unfold before you. Highly successful people are master interpreters. People who have attained greatness have an ability which they have developed to interpret negative or disempowering events as positive challenges which will assist them in growing and moving even farther up the ladder of success. There are no negative experiences only experiences which aid in your development and toughen your character so that you may soar to new heights. There are no failures, only lessons.

22. Take a speed reading course. Reading is a powerful way to gain many years of experience from a few hours of study. For example, most biographies reflect the strategies and philosophies of great leaders or courageous individuals. Read them and model them. Speed reading will allow you to digest large quantities of material in relatively small periods of time.

23. Remember people's names and treat everyone well. This habit, along with enthusiasm, is one of the great success secrets. Everyone in this world wears an imaginary button that screams out "I WANT TO FEEL IMPORTANT AND APPRECIATED!".

24. Be soft as a flower when it comes to kindness but tough as thunder when it comes to principle. Be courteous and polite at all times but never be pushed around. Ensure that you are always treated with respect.

25. Never discuss your health, wealth and other personal matters with anyone outside of your immediate family. Be very disciplined in this regard.

26. Be truthful, patient, persevering, modest and generous.

27. Soak in a warm bath at the end of a long, productive day. Reward yourself for even the smallest of achievement. Take time out for renewal of your mind, body and spirit. Soon all your more important goals will be met and you will move to the next level of peak performance.

28. Learn the power of breathing and its relationship with your energy source. The mind is intimately connected with your breathing. For example, when the mind is agitated, your breathing becomes quick and shallow. When you are relaxed and focused, your breathing is deep and calm. By practising deep, abdominal breathing, you will develop a calm, serene demeanor that will remain cool in the hottest of circumstances. Remember the rule of the Eastern mountain men: "to breathe properly is to live properly."

29. Recognize and cultivate the power of autosuggestion. It works and is an essential tool in maintaining peak performance. We are all performers in one way or another and it is particularly valuable to use such techniques of athletes and public figures for our own enhancement. If you want to become more enthusiastic, repeat "I am more enthusiastic today and am improving this trait daily". Repeat it over and over. Purchase a legal notepad and write out this mantra 500 times. Do it for three weeks with regular practice and feel that this quality is developing. Very soon it will come. This is a strategy that Indian sages have employed for thousands of years to aid their spiritual and mental development. Do not be discouraged if the results are not immediate, they will certainly develop. The spoken word is a powerful influencer of the mind.

30. Maintain a diary to measure your progress and to express your thoughts. Writing out not only your successes but your troubles is one of the world's most effective methods of erasing the worry habit, staying in optimum state and developing precision of thought.

31. Stress is simply a response which you create in the interpretation of an event. Two people might find that a given event results in quite different responses. For example, an after dinner speech might strike fear into the

heart of an inexperienced speaker while a strong orator views it as a wonderful opportunity to share his thoughts. Understanding that the perceived negative effects of an event or task may be mentally manipulated and conditioned towards the positive, will allow you to be a peak performer in all instances.

32. Read "The Seven Habits of Highly Effective People" by Stephen Covey. It contains a wealth of wisdom and powerful insights into further developing your character and enhancing your personal relationships.

33. Become a committed audio-tape user. Most personal-mastery programs and books are now offered in this format. Listen to these inspirational materials on your way to work, whilst waiting in the line at a bank or while you wash dishes in the evening. Make your car a college on wheels and use the drive time to make knowledge your best friend. All down time can be very effectively used in this productive fashion. Use such opportunities to learn and continually expand your mind and its vast potential.

34. Try fasting one day every two weeks. During these fast days, drink fruit juice and eat fresh fruits only. You will feel more energetic, cleansed and alert. Fasting also has a salutary effect on your will-power as you are subverting the otherwise pressing impulses in your mind calling on you to eat more.

35. Keep a radio-cassette player at your office and listen to soft, soothing music throughout the day. Place pleasant scents and inspirational pictures in your workplace. By the magic of association, your work will become something you enjoy even more and arouse a very pleasant feeling within you. Budget your time on trips such that you can spend half an hour in the airport bookstore. They always contain the latest and best self-mastery books and tapes given that those who travel by air are of a group that finds value in these materials.

36. Read "As a Man Thinketh" by James Allen. And don't just read this little book once, read it over and over again. It contains an abundance of timeless wisdom on living a fuller and happier life.

37. Remember that forgiveness is a virtue that few develop, but one that is most important to maintaining peace of mind. Mark Twain wrote that forgiveness is the fragrance the violet sheds on the heel that has crushed it. Practice forgiveness especially in those situations where it is seemingly difficult. By using your emotional forgiveness muscles more regularly, petty wrongs, remarks and slights will not touch you and nothing will penetrate your concentrated, serene mindset.

38. Empty your cup. A full cup cannot accept anything more. Similarly, a person who believes that he cannot learn anything else will stagnate quickly and not move to higher levels. A true sign of a secure, mature individual is someone who sees every opportunity as a chance to learn. Even the teachers have teachers.

39. The Two Minute Mind is an excellent exercise for developing concentration. Simply stare at the second hand on your wristwatch for two minutes and think about nothing else for that time. At first your mind will wander but after 21 days of practice, your attention will not waver during the routine. One of the greatest qualities a person can develop to ensure his success is the ability to focus for extended periods of time. Learn to build up your concentration muscles and no task will be too difficult for you.

40. Drink a cup of warm water before a speech. Ronald Reagan employed this strategy to ensure that he maintained his honey-smooth voice. Mastery of the art of public speaking is a noble goal. So dedicate yourself to it. You will be judged by the calibre of your communication skills.

41. When you stand and meet someone, stand firm and steadfast. A telling sign of an unfocused, weak mind is constant fidgeting, shifting of the eyes and shallow breathing.

42. Act tough and you will be tough. Have courage and inspire others with your actions. But always be considerate.

43. Ask not what this world can do for you but, rather, what you can do for this world. Make service an important goal in your life. It is a most fulfilling investment of time. Remember, in the twilight of your life, when

all is said and done, the quality of your life boils down to the quality of your contribution to others. Leave a rich legacy for those around you to savour.

44. Once a week, arise at dawn. It is a magical time of day. Be still, go for a walk or simply listen to an old Ella Fitzgerald recording. Take a long, hot shower and do 100 pushups. Read one of the classics. You will feel alive and invigorated.

45. Remain slightly aloof. Do not let everyone know everything about you. Cultivate a mystique.

46. Master the art of public speaking. There are few natural speakers. One great trial lawyer stammered dreadfully but through courage and strength of conviction, he developed into a brilliant orator. Role model anyone you think is a highly effective, influential communicator. Visualize a picture of this person. Stand like him, smile like him, and talk like him. The results will startle you.

47. Seek out motivational speakers committed to character training and lifelong success. Make it a point to attend inspirational lectures each month to consistently renew the importance of personal growth in your mind. In a two hour seminar, you can learn powerful techniques and strategies that others have spent many years learning and refining. Never feel that you have no time for gathering new ideas, you are investing in yourself.

48. Read the wonderful book "Discovering Happiness" by Dennis Wholey. It will certainly open up new horizons for you in your quest for an optimal state of health and happiness.

49. To enhance your concentration, read a passage in a book you have never explored. Then try to recite it verbatim. Practice this for only 5 minutes a day and enjoy the results which follow after a few months of effort.

50. Try entering a 5 km running race and then a 10 km event. The adrenaline that flows from the experience of racing with several hundred other fitness-minded people is exhilarating. By constantly pushing the envelope of your capacity, your potential will quickly unfold. Remember, the body will give you only what you ask of it.

51. Aromas have been proven to be an effective means of entering a state of relaxation. Scents have a very noticeable effect on your mindset and moods. Purchase the essential oils of orange and clove bud from your local health food shop. Put a few drops of either oil within a cup of boiling water and inhale the sweet smelling steam for a few minutes. Then let the mixture sit in the room where you are resting. You will gain a sense of peace and serenity. A little apple spice in the air has recently been shown to induce a far more restful sleep.

52. Cultivate the art of walking half an hour after you have finished eating your evening meal. Walks in natural settings are the very best. Walking is, perhaps, nature's ideal exercise. And when you walk, do not think about work or about the bills or about the challenges you might be facing - this will neutralize many of the benefits. Simply enjoy the walk. Notice the richness of your surroundings. Let your senses drink in the beauty of nature and the crispness of the air for a change. So many people who have mastered the art of growing younger have also mastered the habit of a daily walk.

53. Start a program of weight lifting at the gym. Strong people are mentally tough people. As you age, you need not lose your physical nor your mental strength. 75 year-old men are running marathons, 80 year-old women have scaled mountains and 90 year-old grandparents are living rich, productive lives. Whether you are 19 or 93, stay fit, stay motivated and stay passionate about life.

54. Never argue with the person you work for - you will lose more than just the argument.

55. In terms of business attire, dark suits (navy blue and charcoal grey) reflect power, sophistication and authority. Have you ever seen a prime minister or president in a tan suit?

56. Regularly send handwritten notes to your business clients and your other relations to strengthen the bond. Develop a system which reminds you to send something valuable to this network at least once every four months. Send them postcards when you are away on vacation. If you have to buy a few hundred postcards and spend an hour writing, don't worry.

This is an exceptionally good investment of your time. Another idea is to send a recent article of interest to your contacts with a handwritten note saying that you thought this would interest them and that you continue to value their friendship. Relationship building should always be a central focus whether you are a CEO, a student, a salesperson or a parent.

57. Two of the fundamentals for a happy, joyful life are balance and moderation. One must maintain a balance of all activities and do nothing to extremes.

58. Drink Jasmine tea which can be obtained from any Chinese herbal shop. It is excellent for your general health and is very relaxing. Also try placing a few slices of fresh ginger in a cup of hot water for a superb tea that will restore vitality and keep you in a peak physical condition.

59. Remember that effective time management makes you more rather than less flexible. It allows you to do the things that you really want to do rather than the things you really have to do.

60. Do not take personal development books as gospel. Read them and take whatever useful ideas you need. Some people feel they must do everything suggested and take the techniques to extremes. Every book has at least one tool or strategy of benefit. Take what you need and what works for you and discard what doesn't suit you.

61. Become an adventurer. Revitalize your spirit and sense of playfulness. Become a kid again. Once every few months, plan to enjoy a new, thrilling activity such as white water rafting, scuba diving, windsurfing, rockclimbing, joining a martial arts club, sailing, deep sea fishing or camping. This will keep your life in perspective, bring you closer to those you share the activity with and keep you feeling invigorated and young.

62. Spend time with Nature. Natural settings have a powerful effect on your senses which in turn will lead to a sense of renewal, refreshment and peacefulness. Peak performers through the ages have understood the importance of getting back to Nature. Start camping or simply taking quiet walks in the forest. Rest by a sparkling stream. Cultivate your own little garden which will serve as your personal oasis in the middle of a crowded

city. By cultivating a friendship with Nature, you will quickly find more serenity, contentment and richness in your life.

63. Recall the wise saying "mens sana in corpore sano" which means in a sound body rests a sound mind. Never neglect the body which is intimately connected to the mind. This is your temple. Feed it the finest fuels, exercise daily and care for it as you would your prized possession - because it is.

64. Be so strong that nothing interferes with your peace of mind. A well-known boxer was once unhappy. When asked why, he said that he had allowed himself to think a negative thought. Curb your desires and stay centered and focused - it gets easier with practice. You truly cannot afford the luxury of even one negative thought.

65. Do not eat three hours before sleep. This allows for smoother digestion and a more restful sleep. For deeper, more renewing sleep, remember that a daily dose of exercise promotes good sleep as does a period of relaxation an hour before bed. Also do not bring work to bed with you or think about anything which might agitate you. Ease yourself into sleep like a baby being sung a soft, soothing lullaby. And finally, as Leonardo da Vinci said: "a well-spent day brings happy sleep."

66. Be careful about your reputation. If it is good it will take you to the highest of heights. But once tarnished, it will be difficult to retrieve. Always reflect on your course of action. Never do anything you wouldn't be proud to tell your mother about. Have fun always but temper it with common sense and prudence.

67. Find mentors to model who will guide you in your progress. The mistakes of the world have all been made once before - why shouldn't you have the benefit of the experience of others? Find someone who has both courage and consideration for others, someone who is therefore mature. Your mentor must have only your best interests in mind and should be sufficiently senior to offer you good guidance on the subjects you seek assistance with. Everyone needs to feel appreciated and even the busiest of executives will find time to assist a person who respects them and values

their advice.

68. Make a list of all your weaknesses. A truly confident and enlightened person will note a weakness and seek to methodically improve. Bear in mind that even the greatest and most powerful people have weaknesses. Some are better than others in hiding them. On the other hand, get to know your best qualities and cultivate them.

69. Never complain. Be known as a positive, strong, energetic and enthusiastic person. Someone who complains, is cynical and always looks for the negative in everything, will scare people away and rarely will succeed at anything. From a purely psychological viewpoint, things are always created twice: once in the mind and then in reality. Focus on the positive. Be so mentally tough that nothing takes you off your planned course to success. Visualize and firmly believe in what you want. It will most certainly come true.

70. Overlook the weaknesses of your friends. If you look for flaws you will most surely find them. Be mature enough to ignore the petty failings of others and see the good that each one inherently possesses. We can learn from everyone. Everyone has a story to tell, a joke to share and a lesson to learn. Open your mind to this and you will learn a tremendous amount. Friends are so very important to a happy existence - especially those who have shared many experiences and laughs with you. Work hard to make friendships, and all your relationships for that matter, stronger and richer. Call your friends, buy them small gifts of books or other items you believe they might enjoy. The "law of the farm" applies to relationships as well as to the rest of life - you reap what you sow and to have great friends you must first be one.

71. Be kind, considerate and courteous. But also be shrewd and know when to be tough and courageous. This is the mark of a well-defined character and you will surely command respect. It is most useful to read books on friendliness and enhancing relationships by being a good listener, showing others sincere appreciation and refining other interpersonal skills. But, to truly succeed, one must also recognize that worldly wisdom and shrewdness are essential skills to foster. Become an expert in human psychology and be able to read the essence of people. Never be taken advantage of and be aware

of the politics around you. Stay above petty gossiping and office politics but appreciate that they indeed exist and know what goes on behind your back. Every great leader does.

72. Create your image as a highly competent, strong, disciplined, calm and decent individual. Find that crucial balance between working on the image that you project to the rest of the world and your inner character. Create a sense of mystery about yourself as the truly wise never show their hand. Do not tell everyone everything about yourself, your strategies and your aspirations. The successful citizens of this world think thrice before they speak because a word uttered can never be retrieved. Make things look easy and people will say you are naturally gifted. Speak only good things and people will flock to you. Never speak ill of others and all will know you will not malign them behind their backs. Build your character and live a highly principled life.

73. Familiarity breeds contempt is a very good rule. The stars remain far above the Earth. You must keep a distance from all but your closest of relations. Once people see everything of a leader he loses his aura and with it the authority and mystique he may have created. For example, Ronald Reagan was known to many as an excellent leader. He carefully cultivated his image of a folksy, considerate politician who kept the interests of the United States first and foremost in his mind. At gatherings of world leaders, he commanded attention and respect in his dark suits, surrounded by the trappings of power such as political aides, security officers and a convoy of limousines. As soon as he appeared, thoughts of authority and power came to our minds. Did you ever see the President with his shirt off swimming at his pool? How about in his dressing gown after waking up after one of his long sleeps, hair tousled and beard grown? Reagan's handlers never allowed such glimpses because they detract from the perception of authority. The American nation was not exposed to these sights. In the Clinton Era things changed and you saw the President eating Big Macs and wearing baseball caps with a full business suit. Whilst these scenes may be endearing to the public, there is little doubt that President Clinton was more familiar to us, merely another one of us and, unlike the stars above, much closer to the ground.

74. Learn to organize your time. It is incorrect to say that by becoming

a meticulous time manager and living by a carefully defined schedule you become rigid and nonspontaneous. Rather, proper organization allows one to accomplish those goals which are truly important as well as enjoy leisure time. Good time management offers more time for fun and relaxation - not less. These important periods are scheduled into the week just like other commitments which may appear more pressing. Neither are sacrificed. Also, discipline yourself and stop wasting time on all those immediate and pressing but unimportant tasks (i.e., the ringing phones) and concentrate on the activities that are truly meaningful to your life's mission. Such activities include time for self-renewal and reflection, time forging relationships built on trust and mutual respect, time for physical fitness, time to read and think deeply and time serving others in your community.

75. Keep well-informed about current events, the latest books and popular trends. Many peak performers read five or six papers a day. You don't have to read every story of every paper. Know what to focus on, what to pass by and what to clip out and read at another time (many successful people scan scores of magazines and papers, clipping out articles of interest; these articles go into a file folder which can be read in your down time). Knowledge is power. Whether you are an entrepreneur, a corporate leader or someone leading a family, you can profoundly change your life and the lives of those around you with a single idea. Just ask Gates, Edison and Bell.

76. When choosing your life partner, remember that this is the most important decision of your lifetime. The marriage relationship offers 90% of all your support, happiness and fulfillment so choose it wisely. Consider qualities such as affection, sense of humor, intelligence, integrity, maturity, temperament, compatibility and that indescribable characteristic of chemistry. If these are present, your relationship stands an excellent chance of great success. Move slowly and let no one press you into an uncomfortable decision.

77. Never discuss your personal development activities with anyone. Your strategies for expanding your mind and spirit are your own. Others might not understand the value of personal-mastery and, further, will take away your credit when you meet with success by saying that you relied on techniques. Keep these self-development activities to yourself.

78. Schedule relaxation time into your week and be ruthless in protecting it. You would not schedule another activity into the time planned for an important meeting with the president of your company or your best client so why would you put off a period to invest in yourself? We must have time for ourselves to reflect, unwind and recharge our batteries. These are the renewal activities that allow us to maintain peak performance and are exceptionally valuable periods.

79. 83% of our sensory input comes from our eyes. To truly concentrate on something, shut your eyes and you will remove much distraction.

80. Be the master of your will but the servant of your conscience.

81. Develop the wonderful habit of a daily swim. It will promote excellent health, keep you relaxed and concentrated, lean and trim. Swimming is not stressful on the body, provides a great workout for the lungs and requires little time to do effectively. Remember that in a fit body resides a fit mind.

82. People who are doing good today are ensuring their happiness for tomorrow.

83. The key to successful time management is doing what you planned to do when you planned to do it. Keep your mind fully on the task at hand. Only then will you achieve all your goals and have time for the things that matter most. Although it is imperative to be flexible (a bow too tightly strung will soon break), following your planned schedule requires no more than simple discipline.

84. An excellent visualization technique: if you are worrying about something, picture the words of your worry on a piece of paper. Now ignite a match to the paper and watch the worry dissipate into flames. Bruce Lee, the great martial arts master employed this mental control device regularly.

85. Compartmentalize your worry. Set aside a certain amount of time to ponder over a problem and map out an effective plan of attack and your options. Once this is done, have the mental fortitude not to come back to the problem and go over it again and again. The human mind is a strange creature - things we want to forget keep coming back and those things we

want to remember are not there when we want them. But the mind is similar to a muscle and the more you flex it the stronger it will become. Make it your servant. Feed it only the best nutrition and information. It will serve you well and perform magic if you believe in it.

86. Peak performers are physically relaxed and mentally engaged.

87. To be at your performance peak mentally, your body must be loose physically and relaxed. It is now beyond dispute that there is a mind-body connection and when the body is supple, free from tension, the mind is clear, calm and focused as well. This is why yoga is such a beneficial activity. It keeps the body relaxed so that the mind can follow. Basic stretching for 15 minutes a day is also an excellent way to release tension that builds up as a result of our life in this highly complex and fast moving, but wonderful world. Try having a massage or power lounging in a Jacuzzi. Relax the body and you relax the mind.

88. Prepare a detailed financial plan for the next few years and follow it. Seek out financial advice if you need it. A powerful strategy for financial mastery is also a simple one: save 10% of all you make for long-term growth (take this off the pay cheque before you have a chance to spend it). If you can invest $200 a month for the next 30 years at an annual return rate of 15%, you will end up with $1.4 million dollars. Being wise with your money is one of the very best investments to make. Financial security leads to personal freedom.

89. Readers are leaders. U.S. President Bill Clinton read more than 300 books during his short time at Oxford University. Some top performers read a book a day. Seek out knowledge and information. We have truly entered the age of massive information and those who are proactive can use this to their advantage. The more you know, the less you fear.

90. Get into the excellent habit of reading something positive and inspirational before you go to bed and as soon as you awake in the morning. You will soon note the benefits as these thoughts will be supporting you throughout the day.

91. Make it one of your goals to develop a dynamic, charismatic personality.

Such a quality is something each one of us has the potential to develop but few do. President Kennedy was a sickly youth but rose above his physical problems to be the most charismatic and exciting political figure in the history of the United States. Start off small. Take a Dale Carnegie course on public speaking. Go to the library where you will find books on the fine art of conversation and personal grooming. Learn three clean and witty jokes and get in the habit of socializing. You will have fun and build a lasting network of friends and associates.

92. On the subject of conversation, a Chinese proverb states as follows: "a single conversation across the table with a wise man is worth a month's study of books." Seek out the wise and learn from them. They are just waiting for that small spark of interest to tell you all that you need to know.

93. Lao-Tzu prized three essential qualities for a person of greatness: "the first is gentleness; the second is frugality; the third is humility, which keeps me from putting myself before others. Be gentle and you can be bold; be frugal and you can be liberal; avoid putting yourself before others and you can become a leader among men."

94. "When you cannot make up your mind which of two evenly balanced courses of action you should take - choose the bolder," said W. J. Slim. There is no substitute for courage and though the chance of stubbing your toe increases the more you walk, it is always better than going nowhere by standing still. Take chances, take smart risks and you will meet with success beyond your dreams.

95. Become your spouse's number one supporter, the one who is always there supporting and fueling hopes and dreams. Develop together and march confidently through the world as an army of two.

96. Think of three people who can provide you with inspiration, motivation and support for your goals and aspirations. Plan to meet with each one of them over the next few weeks. Listen enthusiastically to them and brainstorm with them. Map out a strategy and take their wise counsel.

97. Make every one of your days a true masterpiece. Remember the old saying: "it's not who you think you are that holds you back but what you

think you're not."

98. Just as valuable energy is wasted by spending time on activities that are of no value, energy can be wasted on loose thinking. Imagine that your mind has an energy measure of 1000 watts at its disposal. Each time your mind wanders off the project at hand, to a nagging worry, to all the things to do by the end of the day, 100 watts is lost. Quite soon the entire energy supply is gone. This is the nature of the mind. Fail to discipline it and your energy levels will be depleted and your accomplishments will be minimal. Control it and you will see great things happening. You will feel more powerful and achieve difficult tasks with ease. The 19th century philosopher Henri Frederic Amiel summed it up nicely: "for purposes of action, nothing is more useful than narrowness of thought combined with energy of will."

99. It has been rightly said that "you sow an action, you reap a habit. You sow a habit, you reap a character. You sow a character, you reap a destiny." The essence of a person is his character - make yours unique, unblemished and strong. Do not say you will do anything unless you will indeed do it. Speak the truth and measure your words wisely. Be humble, straightforward and peaceful.

100. Remember the overriding law of nature: positive overcomes the negative.

101. A contented mind is a continual feast. Greed and material desires must be curbed to achieve lasting happiness and serenity. Be happy with what you have. Do you really need all of those material possessions? One can develop contentment just as one develops patience, courage and concentration - with daily practice and sincere desire.

102. Make a new friend or acquaintance every day. Keep an updated list of all contacts close at hand. Rich relationships are the DNA of a rich, rewarding life.

103. Remember this ancient Indian proverb: "if you conquer your mind, you conquer the world."

104. Place greater importance on staying happy than amassing material possessions. A zest for life is developed and carefully nurtured through thoughtful activities and pursuits.

105. Contrary to popular opinion, stress is not a bad thing. It allows us to perform at peak levels and can assist us through the flood of chemicals it releases within our bodies. What is harmful is too much stress, or more particularly, a lack of relief from stress. The times of stress must be balanced nicely with times of pure relaxation and leisure for us to be healthy and at our best. Many of the great leaders of our time were exposed to crushing workloads and the burdens of high office. But they prospered by developing strategies to balance the challenging times with fun and calming times. President Kennedy would have regular naps in his White House office. Winston Churchill had the same practice and slept for one hour every afternoon to stay alert, focused and calm. Not only is it essential to be physically relaxed to maintain optimal health but one must couple this trait with mental serenity. Too often people think that vigorous exercise, good nutrition and pleasant leisure activities will be the panacea for all ills. These pursuits must be combined with positive thinking and peace of mind for true happiness and longevity.

106. Get into the habit of taking mental vacations throughout the day. Visit Bermuda for five minutes in the morning. Visualize a swim in the Mediterranean in the afternoon and skiing down the slopes of the Alps just before you head for home at the end of your busy and productive day. Try this for two months and schedule these rest periods into your agenda just as you would your essential meetings or tasks. The rewards will be significant.

107. A change is as good as a rest. Whether this change is as major as a change of employment or as minor as a leisure pursuit which occupies your entire attention for an hour three times a week, these changes in routine, and mindset are entirely beneficial. In selecting the activity, try to find something totally engaging which requires deep concentration so that your mind is free from the mundane but seemingly important aspects of your day. Many executives are becoming involved in the martial arts for just this reason. If your mind wanders for even a split second, a harsh lesson is soon learned. Pain is a great motivator and always will be.

108. Study these 10 fundamentals of happiness:

i. Pursue a productive, exciting and active life.
ii. Engage in meaningful activities every minute of every day.
iii. Develop an organized, planned lifestyle with little chaos.
iv. Set realistic goals yet keep your mark high.
v. Think positively - you cannot afford the luxury of a negative thought.
vi. Avoid needless worry over trifling matters.
vii. Devote time to fun.
viii. Develop a warm, outgoing personality with a sincere love of people.
ix. Get in the habit of giving more than receiving.
x. Learn to live in the present. The past is water under the bridge of life.

109. Strive to be humble and live a simple life.

110. Read "A History of Knowledge" by Charles Van Doren which chronicles the history of the world's ideas. In this one book is an absolute wealth of knowledge. Get it, read it and enjoy it.

111. Read "The Art of the Leader" by William A. Cohen. It is both inspirational and practical.

112. Develop that elusive quality known as charisma. The following are ten qualities of a Charismatic leader:

• Be committed to what you are doing.
• Look like a winner and act like one.
• Have big dreams, a vision and reach for the sky.
• Steadily advance in the direction of your goals.
• Prepare and work hard at every task you do.
• Build a mystique around yourself.
• Be interested in others and show kindness.
• Have a strong sense of humour.
• Be known for the strength of your character.
• Have grace under pressure. (John F. Kennedy said that "the elusive half-step between middle management and true leadership is grace under pressure.")

113. In work, love and life, play hard and play fair.

114. Do not talk when you are listening. Interrupting is one of the most common discourtesies. Listen aggressively with the full scope of your attention. You will be amazed at what you learn and how your counsel will soon be sought by many.

115. "Anybody can become angry - that is easy; but to be angry with the right person, and to the right degree, and at the right time, and for the right purpose, and in the right way - that is not within everybody's power and is not easy." - Aristotle

116. Knowledge is power. People who have achieved great success are not necessarily more skillful or intelligent than others. What separates them is their burning desire and thirst for knowledge. The more one knows, the more one achieves. Great leaders have techniques to allow them to arrive at the top of the mountain. Read the biographies of the world's leaders and learn from their habits, inspirations and philosophies. Cultivate the important practice of active role modelling.

117. All the answers to any questions are in print. How to improve as a public speaker, how to improve your relations with others, how to become fitter or develop a better memory - all aspects of personal development are dealt with in books. Therefore, in order to achieve your maximum potential, you must read daily. But, in this age of information, you must be ruthless in what you consume. Focus on your goals and read only those materials that will be an asset to you. Do not attempt to read everything for you are busy and have other tasks at hand. Choose what is important and filter out what is of no value. Begin with a solid newspaper every morning for an excellent summary of the key events of the day. Also ensure that your readings are broadly based. For example, perhaps you may wish to read history, business, Eastern philosophy, health books etc. Then go to the library and develop the habit of making regular visits. Read the classics from Hemingway to Bram Stoker. Read history, with all its lessons on life and read biology for a new perspective. Look under the heading of "success" at the library and you will be amazed at the literature you will find: inspirational stories of people who developed greatness in the face of adversity, strategies for improving

yourself physically, mentally and spiritually and texts to tap the unlimited power for success that certainly exists within us. Drink deeply from such books. Surround yourself with them and read them constantly whether on the bus each day or before you go to bed. Let them inspire and motivate you.

118. Get into the habit of breakfast meetings. An early meal to touch base with a friend or business associate is a most pleasant way to start the day and allows you to maintain your contacts in the face of a busy schedule.

119. If you live in a flat, always ensure that it is very bright and has a swimming pool. A pool is especially important because it will allow you to exercise no matter how busy your schedule. There is nothing like a refreshing swim after a long, productive day. You will feel excellent and sleep like a baby.

120. "Excellence is an art won by training and habituation. We do not act rightly because we have virtue or excellence, but rather we have those because we have acted rightly. We are what we repeatedly do. Excellence, then, is not an act but a habit." - Aristotle

121. "Today is yesterday's pupil." - Benjamin Franklin

122. If you have a choice of taking two paths, always take the more daring of the two. Calculated risk taking often produces extraordinary results.

123. Every day, get away from the noise, the crowds and the rush and spend a few hours alone in peaceful introspection, deep reading or simple relaxation.

124. That which any person who has walked this Earth has achieved you can achieve with the right mental attitude, perseverance and industry. Limiting thoughts and weak mental images must be banished. One's focus must be on the attainment of goals that are truly important.

125. Get into the habit of memorizing beautiful poetry. Not only will it be a great source of entertainment but it will quickly lift your intellectual functions to a higher level by improving your memory, concentration and mental agility.

126. Keep your words soft and arguments hard.

127. Break the worry habit by putting things in perspective and laughing over small setbacks. Repeat to yourself that "this will soon pass". Then take a sheet of paper, write out the worry on your mind. Allot a certain period of time to think on it, isolate the precise problem and formulate a powerful line of attack. By this practical technique, your negative, energy sapping habit will soon be a faint memory of the past.

128. Be known as that person who goes the extra mile. The person who works longer than others. The one who takes on the extra assignments and follows them through with great success. Be the person who always has concerns about others and who makes family members feel truly special. Be a standout, the one with a balance in both personal and professional excellence. Be a star that shines brightly for all others to admire.

129. Become a committed and sincere networker. Cultivate new friendships. You will truly be surprised where people end up over the years and how small, kind gestures will help you later on in life. Treat everyone who crosses your path as if they are the most important person in your world. You will certainly meet with great success.

130. When you look for something you will find it. If you constantly expect exceptional success, you will surely have it. Peak performers attract success. You must keep the goals you desire to achieve at the forefront of your mind throughout the day. Repeat your ambitions at least five times a day and visualize yourself achieving them. If your goal is to be rich, picture the house you will be living in, the car you will be driving, what it will feel like to be rich and the pleasure of attaining your goals in life. Repeat your ambition over and over until you have complete certainty that you will attain your desires and eventually you will.

131. Develop a sense of wonder about the world. Be an explorer. Find pleasure in the things that others take for granted. Stop and actually listen to that wonderful street musician playing the trumpet. Read that classic book your father loved so much. Plan to get away from the city next week and visit a secluded, powerfully natural place for a few days. Take a mini-retreat

and care for your mind, body and spirit. It will profoundly improve the quality of your life.

132. Send cards on birthdays and little notes from time to time showing that you care and were thinking about your relations. We are all busy but if you spend just five minutes a week to send a card to a friend or family member, by the year end you will have sent out 52 cards. This is a small investment for the dividends that are guaranteed to follow.

133. Remember and use people's names when you talk to them. A person's name is a uniquely sweet sound to them.

134. Go outdoors and look up into the blue sky for half an hour. Note the supremely strong feeling that you get when you are connected to Nature. Get away from your rigid schedule today and spend the afternoon in a beautiful setting. Walk in the woods and sit by a cool stream. Go fishing or rent a canoe. Getting away from your routine will provide a refreshing release and make you feel wonderful when you eventually return.

135. Once every few weeks, leave your watch at home. In this society we often become bound to the clock and soon it governs our every action like a rigid taskmaster. Go through the day doing precisely what you wish to do and for however long you wish to do it. Spend time with that special person without having to run off to your next appointment. Savour the moments and focus on what is truly important rather than those mundane things that somehow take on a greater importance than they really deserve. Lose the clock and gain some quality time.

136. Laugh at work and be known as a positive achiever.

137. An idea gives rise to a mental image. A mental image will then generate a mental habit out of which a mental trait ultimately blossoms. Master your thoughts and you master your mind; master your mind and you master your life; master your life and you master your destiny.

138. Recognize the tremendous power of opposition thinking. This simple technique simply involves the substitution of a positive thought each and every time a negative or limiting thought enters your mind and begins

to detract from your focus. For example, on a Sunday evening, you may think "I wish I did not have to return to work tomorrow after such a pleasant and relaxing weekend." Immediately replace this defeating thought pattern before it begins to take hold by thinking the opposite. For example you might think "I cannot wait to return to the office given the exciting projects on the go and the wonderful sense of accomplishment I receive after a productive, challenging week." Then think how fortunate you are to have a job and one that you can advance in through your own efforts and productivity. Make a list of all of the positive attributes of your position and repeat them over and over. Soon the negative pattern will be broken and you will look toward the exciting week ahead with that most fabulous of qualities: enthusiasm.

139. Get deep into the habit of personal introspection. Ben Franklin called this one of the most important strategies for personal effectiveness. Spend ten minutes every night before you go to bed in self-examination. Think about the good things you did during the day and the bad actions you may have taken which you must change in order to excel and grow. Successful people are simply more thoughtful than others. Daily reflection will soon allow for the eradication of your negative qualities (ranging from procrastination to gossiping to insulting others) and will sharpen the mind. After steady practice, a time will eventually arrive when the mistakes you make are few indeed and your personal power will move to the highest level.

140. The most efficient and effective alarm clock ever developed lies within our own minds. If you do not believe this, try the following: 1. Sit in an easy chair approximately ten minutes before you go to bed. 2. Shut your eyes and gently rest your hands on your knees. 3. Breathe deeply for a few minutes (inhale to the count of five, hold to the count of ten and exhale fully). 4. Repeat the following command to yourself at least twenty times: "I will awake at (the desired time) feeling fresh, alert and enthusiastic." This command must be said with feeling and emotion. Then take a few seconds to visualize yourself waking up at the desired time (the more detailed the mental picture the better) and imagine how great you will feel. You will soon wake up at the desired moment after little or no practice.

141. Some men see things as they are and say "why?" I dream of things that never were and say "why not?" George Bernard Shaw

142. Use these strategies to improve the quality of your mind-calming meditation: 1. Practice meditation at the same time each day and in the same place so that your mind becomes accustomed to entering the desired serene state as soon as you enter the peaceful place. 2. The early morning is undoubtedly the most powerful time to meditate. Indian yogis believe that the pre-dawn time has almost magical qualities which aid in achieving the super-peaceful state so many meditators attempt to attain. 3. Before you start, command your mind to be quiet by using affirmations such as "I will be focused and very calm now." 4. If thoughts do enter, do not force them out but simply let them pass like clouds making way for the beautiful blue sky. Picture that your mind is like a still lake without even a ripple. 5. Sit for ten minutes at first and then increase the time every few sittings. After a month or two, you will not be interrupted by any pressing thoughts and will surely feel a sense of peace that you have never felt before.

143. Forge and foster great friendships as such relationships are essential for maintaining a healthy and successful life. Find a few minutes every day to jot down some warm wishes to an old friend or to place a telephone call to someone you have not had a chance to speak to for a while. Show compassion and sincere consideration for all your friends and watch the results which follow. Develop long lasting friendships by being a good friend. Also, make it a priority to seek out new friends no matter how many you may be fortunate enough to have. This is one of life's greatest joys which many of us miss.

144. Purchase a cassette or CD of Miles Davis's Kind Of Blue. It is a uniquely soothing compilation that will refresh and soothe you after a challenging and productive day. Music such as this is good for the soul.

145. Drown your appetite by drinking more water - ten glasses a day is ideal. It revitalizes the system and purifies the body. Also, get into the habit of eating soups and more complex carbohydrates such as rice, potatoes and pasta which feed your hunger with far less calories than other less healthy foods. You truly are what you eat and must ensure that your diet is designed to maximize your energy and mental clarity.

146. Develop the essential habit of punctuality for it is most important for high success. Punctuality reflects discipline and a proper regard for others. Without it, even the most sophisticated person appears slightly offensive. Do not be early and certainly never be late. Budget your time and, should you arrive early, take a walk or simply relax for a few moments to ensure that you arrive on time as requested. You will be appreciated and welcomed always if you cultivate this important quality that appears so rarely these days.

147. The telephone is there for your convenience, not for the convenience of others who are attempting to contact you. If you are busy with a task, do not answer the phone or have someone answer the call so that you may return it at a more suitable time. Do not let such interruptions waste your time. Most phone calls are not important and last far too long anyway. Over the course of the average American's lifetime, she will spend two years unsuccessfully returning phone calls. There are so many important and fun things to do in life. The challenge is to respect precious time so that we can achieve a fuller, more satisfying life.

148. Start your day off well. Before you get out of bed each morning, say a prayer or repeat your personal affirmation giving thanks for the day and all the positive things you will see and achieve. Make a conscious decision to make this the best day of your life and meet with pleasure, success and fun. If you believe it, it will most certainly happen. A timeless secret for lifelong success is to live each day as if it were your last.

149. Confide in your partner. This will strengthen the relationship and allow you both to grow at the same pace. It is also a wonderful tonic to share important or otherwise troubling things with the person you are closest to.

150. Push yourself just a little harder and a little farther each day. Winners on the playing field of life push the envelope of their potential daily. Do the thing you fear and the death of fear is certain. Winners do the things that less developed people don't like doing even though they also might not enjoy doing them. This is what strength of character and courage is all about. Tackle your weaknesses. Do the thing that you have consistently put off. Write that thank you note or letter that you have neglected for so long.

Exercise your discipline muscles and they will rise to the occasion by filling your day with more satisfaction, more effectiveness and far more energy.

151. All individuals who have attained the highest of levels generally have cultivated the essential mental habit of optimism. Without optimism, life loses its lustre and hardships appear at every step of the way. This is an essential life habit.

152. Today, write down the seven best qualities of individuals who you admire and post this list by your bed. Then, each morning as you rise, focus on a new quality which you will strive to implement during the day. After one week, you will notice small differences in yourself. In one month, these traits will become firmly embedded. After two months, all those important qualities will be yours.

153. You have as many reputations as you do acquaintances as each person you know thinks differently of you. What should truly concern you is your character. You have full control of this and this is what you must develop, refine and cultivate. Once your character is strong and vigorous, then all else that is positive will follow.

154. Consider yourself as an orange. Only what is really inside can come out. If you fill your mind with thoughts of serenity, positivity, strength, courage and compassion, when someone squeezes you, this is the only juice that can flow.

155. Our lives have been described as a parenthesis in eternity. We are but a small blip on the stage of the Universe. As we can take nothing with us when we leave, then the real meaning of our existence must be to give and serve others. Keep this in mind. When you wake up early in the morning, repeat the mantra: "I will serve others today, I will care for others today and I will be kind today." This kind of living will bring you huge returns if you stay on the purpose of aiding others rather than on the outcome of personal gain.

156. Be known as an innovator at your place of work. Sit down over the next week and write out ten suggestions for your supervisor as to how to improve the work being done and the quality of the workplace itself. Be

known as an idea person willing to discover challenges and tackle them with zest and enthusiasm.

157. Learn to laugh at yourself.

158. Keep open the windows of your mind.

159. Try to go through one full day without saying "I". Focus on others. Listen to others and you will learn wonderful new things as well as gain friendships.

160. Spend one hour a day in full silence except in answer to direct questions. Even then, answer directly and without extending the conversation unduly. We, so very often, talk around subjects and repeat ourselves. This ancient Eastern exercise will not only build your will-power but develop clarity and precision of language which is essential for effective communication.

161. Each day, do two things that you do not like doing. This may be the preparation of a report you have been putting off or shining your shoes. It does not matter how small the task, just do it! Soon these chores will not seem so bad, your personal power will increase and your productivity will soar. Try it because this is an age-old technique for building strength of character.

162. True happiness comes from only one thing: achievement of goals, whether they are personal, professional or otherwise. You are happiest when you feel you are growing. When you feel that you are contributing and advancing in the direction of your dreams, you will notice that you have boundless energy and vitality. Time spent on activities which offer little reward aside from a fleeting feeling of relaxation (television watching is the best example), is time lost forever. Relaxation is essential but chose the most effective means of renewal and spend your time in productive pursuits that will slowly move you along the path of accomplishment. Happiness comes from doing - not sleeping.

163. Napoleon III of France had a special ability to remember the names of all those he met. His secret was to say "so sorry, I missed your name"

after being introduced to a new person. This would cause the name to be repeated and reinforced within his memory. If the name was difficult, he would ask for the proper spelling.

164. The sages of China have held a basic life philosophy for thousands of years: develop an indomitable spirit along with courtesy and integrity. The repetition of these three traits will make you an exceptionally powerful individual respected by all. Exert your effort and personal influence to attain these qualities.

165. A valuable technique for defeating negative and self-limiting thoughts that can hamper you from attaining peak performance is the mental interrupt device. When a negative thought enters your consciousness, first you must become aware of it and have a strong desire to remove it for good. To do this, interrupt the negative train of thought by doing something to break and banish the self-limiting pattern. When the bad thought enters, you may pinch yourself and say, "I am strong and weak thoughts are gone", or you may shout out loud or do anything that will divert your attention and remove the negative focus. By practising this technique, you will see a marked decrease in the negative thoughts that most people have, paving the way to the mindset of a true winner.

166. Taking time from your busy work and family schedule to focus on personal growth activities is essential and is never to be considered a waste. Taking one hour from your hectic morning to watch kids playing in a nearby park or to take a brisk walk might seem like a poor use of time to some. But by making more time for life's simple pleasures and bringing more balance into your day, you will make the remaining hours far more productive and effective. You cannot do good unless you feel good. When you are serene, relaxed and enthusiastic you are also more productive, creative and dynamic. This is something that has been proved time and time again and yet we consistently get caught up in the apparent immediacy of our routine and fail to see the forest for the trees.

167. Read more, learn more, laugh more and love more.

168. Pick five relationships that you desire to improve over the next six months. Write out the names of these people and under each name detail

why you want to improve the relationship, how you plan to do so and in what time frame. This is simply another facet of goal setting - the practice which will always yield excellent results in any of life's fields. Be committed to being a better parent, friend and citizen. Be creative in the steps you take to show your appreciation and respect for your loved ones. Sending notes is fine but consider unique and thoughtful measures ranging from a romantic picnic in the country with your partner to an early morning fishing trip with an old friend.

169. Remember the power of prayer.

170. An excellent investment in your personal growth is the six tape series of Reverend Norman Vincent Peale entitled "The Power of Positive Thinking". Get it and listen to it over and over. It is packed full of strategies and techniques that, without fail, will ensure that you live a long, happy, productive and prosperous life.

171. Consider purchasing a pocket organizer which may prove to be an excellent tool for scheduling, recording your commitments and keeping the responsibilities of your life in fine order. One can be purchased at a reasonable price.

172. Browse second-hand bookstores every few months searching for lost treasures of character-building books. You will find gems on public speaking, improving your habits, time management, personal health and other important subjects for low prices. Some of these older texts are the very best and come from an age where every young person was under an obligation to develop discipline and good life habits regularly.

173. Read The Magic of Believing by Claude M. Bristol. It will allow you to release the powerful forces which most certainly exist in your mind but may presently be untapped.

174. Be known as someone with a cool head, warm heart and great character. Your presence on this earth will long be remembered.

175. It has been said that doing something for others is the highest form of religion. Every week, out of the 168 hours available, spend a few in service

to others. Many say that such selfless service soon becomes a key focus within their lives. Give your time at a seniors home or to needy children. Teach someone how to read or offer to give a public lecture on the subject of your expertise. Simply take action and do something to leave a legacy.

176. Fill your home with bright, fresh flowers. This is one of the best investments you can make. Let the sounds of great music, loud laughter and good fun fill the oasis of your home.

177. Get to know and enjoy your neighbors. They make life more pleasant and can provide helpful resources when you least expect it.

178. Recognize the power of mantras and the repetition of positive, powerful words. Indian yogis have employed this technique for over 4000 years to live tranquil, productive and focused lives. Create your own personal mantra which you can repeat daily to enhance your character and strengthen your spirit.

179. When the breath is still and strong, so is the mind.

180. Use the following visualization from time to time. Sit in a quiet place and picture that you will be on the earth for only another day. Who would you call, what would you say and what would you do? These questions will give you some important insights into what outstanding actions you must endeavor to complete.

181. Study the following evidence of high character:

• Precision & clarity of thought and speech
• Refined and gentle manners
• The power and habit of introspection
• The power of personal growth
• The power to achieve your goals & dreams

182. "Youth is not a time of life; it is a state of mind. People grow old only by deserting their ideals and by outgrowing the consciousness of youth. Years wrinkle the skin, but to give up enthusiasm wrinkles the soul... You are as old as your doubt, your fear, your despair. The way to keep young is to keep

your faith young. Keep your self-confidence young. Keep your hope young."
- Dr. L.F. Phelan

183. Explore the healing powers of Chinese herbal medicine and similar Eastern strategies for maintaining a state of perfect health (consult an expert at all times and take a formal course on the subject to gain powerful insights into this most useful area of healing).

184. Be certain to organize your time around the true priorities of your life. As Stephen Covey has noted: "it is easy to say no when there is a deeper yes burning within."

185. Slow down your pace of life. In this complex age, we are running our lives at a frantic pace. Focus on what is truly important and start undertaking activities that will slow you down and rekindle the natural, calm within us. Sit in the grass and watch the blue sky for half an hour - at first, it is not as easy as one would think and the urge is to get up after only a few minutes of such useful relaxation. Once you are used to a healthier pace of living, with regular periods dedicated to the simple pleasures of life, every other activity will become more efficient and enjoyable.

186. Try eating only fruit and milk for a full day. Fasting is a powerful success strategy of the East that millions use regularly to maintain peak health and mental clarity. By trying this simple practice every few weeks you will notice a surge in your energy level and a lightness in your walk. Big meals require a significant amount of energy that could be better directed toward more productive pursuits.

187. Value your spouse's laugh and keep your partner's picture close by your work desk for inspiration and pleasant thoughts throughout the day.

188. If you are married, have your partner's initials and your own engraved on the inside of your wedding bands along with the date of your marriage. This is useful not only in case the rings are lost but to provide you both with personalized keepsakes that may be passed down to successive generations.

189. The mind is like a garden - as you sow, so shall you reap. When you cultivate it and nurture it, it will blossom beyond your wildest expectation. But if you let the weeds take over, you will never reach your potential. What you put in is what you get out. So avoid violent movies, trashy novels and all other negative influences. Peak performers are meticulous about the thoughts they allow into the gardens of their minds. You truly cannot afford the luxury of a single negative thought.

190. Do a hundred sit ups a day and do not break this habit. Strong abdominal muscles are very helpful to ensuring that you enjoy peak health and injury free days. They also maintain your appearance and confidence level.

191. Be the most honest person that you know. Be trustworthy - worthy of the trust of others.

192. Curb your worldly desires and you will strengthen your will. He who is deeply bound to material things runs into difficulty and unhappiness when they are taken away. Happy people enjoy worldly objects but do not become bound or wedded to them. Live a simple, uncluttered and productive existence. To simplify your life today, consider selling your television, stopping the junk mail, spending less, learning yoga, selling your car, practising meditation every morning and unplugging your ringing phone once in a while.

193. If you have not laughed today, you have not lived today. Laugh hard and loud. As William James said: "we don't laugh because we are happy, we are happy because we laugh."

194. Read The Charisma Factor - How to Develop Your Natural Leadership Ability by Robert J. Richardson and S. Katharine Thayer. It is a superb book for any aspiring leader, or a current one, who seeks to advance to the next level.

195. Travel often. The perspective offered by visiting new lands is important and allows one to appreciate the existence that we generally take for granted.

196. Each month set a physical fitness goal for yourself. Start to swim in July or learn to ski in January. The key is to arrive at a goal for the month, write it down, consider how to execute it and then, as the NIKE ad says: "Just Do It!".

197. Things are always created twice. There is always the mental creation which precedes the physical creation. Just as plans for a house must first be set down on paper before the house is started, so too should your day be planned within your mind early in the morning before the day begins. Visualize the wonders you desire this life to bring and they will materialize as your subconscious mind starts to focus on the attainment of goals. This is a true law of Nature.

198. Walk to work and notice the wonderful beauty in Nature.

199. Sleep less, spend less, do more, live longer and be greater.

200. Read these over and over and share it with others!